BEYOND THE CROSS

HENRY MCQUEEN

Order this book online at www.trafford.com
or email orders@trafford.com

Most Trafford titles are also available at major online book retailers.

Note for Librarians: A cataloguing record for this book is available from Library
and Archives Canada at www.collectionscanada.ca/amicus/index-e.html

Printed in Victoria, BC, Canada.

ISBN: 978-1-4251-9187-0 (sc)

*Our mission is to efficiently provide the world's finest, most
comprehensive book publishing service, enabling every author to
experience success. To find out how to publish your book, your way, and
have it available worldwide, visit us online at www.trafford.com*

Trafford rev. 8/28/2009

 www.trafford.com

North America & international
toll-free: 1 888 232 4444 (USA & Canada)
phone: 250 383 6864 ♦ fax: 812 355 4082

Prologue

This story was written by someone who knew he had something to share with the world.

This story exposes the truth as to what actually happened to Jesus after he was taken down from the cross. It starts with the life of a young boy who feels somewhat ostracized. It tells of his search for the truth and his ongoing battle with society's obsession with getting people to conform. His search takes him through various religions and culminates in his shattering discovery of what really happened after the crucifixion.

Please note that with the exception of family and a few close friends names have been changed to protect innocent people.

Reader beware! Some of the contents of this fact based story may shock you. People of certain religious convictions may even find it downright unacceptable. Keep an open mind. Accept what you feel is fair and reasonable. If you feel like crucifying the author it is too late. He died just the other day.

Acknowledgements

Thank you to those who stood by me during the good times and the bad. Thank you for your well intended criticism. You will no doubt be happy that I did take some of your advice.

Thanks to my dear wife for your understanding and support.

Thanks to Juanita Kaatz for typing the basic draft of this story and not crucifying me for it.

Thanks to my son Henry for accepting me as I am.

Thanks to my daughter Juanita for designing the front cover.

Thanks to my friend Heinz Kramer for prodding me to go on when I was ready to quit.

Thanks to the good doctor and pathologist who helped research and substantiate the medical facts contained in the manuscript.

Thank you to Jean Sharrocks and Phyl Rowe for proof reading the original manuscript.

Thank you to Rinada van Niekerk for insisting that I do proper research to back up what may otherwise have come over as mere conjecture.

Thank you to Amy and Karen for their publishing guidance and advice.

Thank you to God for letting the truth be known to all mankind.

Contents

```
     ----------------
       =          =
       =          =
       =          =
       =          =
       =          =
-------------------------------------------------------------
 =       HERE LIES JOHN EDMONDSON              =
 =            Born 01-12-1941                   =
 =            Died 15-03-2009                   =
 =       May his soul rest in peace            =
-------------------------------------------------------------
       =          =
       =          =
       =          =
       =          =
       =          =
       =          =
       =          =
       =          =
       =          =
       =          =
       =          =
       =          =
       =          =
     ----------------
```

Chapter One

John Edmondson

John Edmonson died last year.
He was a white South African of Calvanistic Scottish descent and therein lies a tale as you shall see.

John Edmondson wanted to make a difference. He wanted to do something profound. John Edmonson had a passion to change the world.

This is his story.

He first became aware of his existence - his separateness from others - at the age of five. Until then life had just been a blending in of his surroundings - his mother, his father, his brother, the trees, the dogs, the hens, the chickens.

John Edmondson had a passion for art. He liked drawing and colouring in pictures. He was part of a very poor family and was much loved and cared for by his parents but teased and bullied by his brother, four years his senior.

One day his mother entered a picture he had coloured in into a competition. He won a prize. The prize was another more detailed drawing which needed colouring in but which according to the judges had to be coloured in according to their rules…. a blue shirt for the boy, a pink skirt for the girl, and so on…. and of course, all within the lines drawn by their artist.

Well, John Edmondson was keen to get started and went at it… hammer and tongs… until his loving mother intervened. He had never seen her angry before but she was so cross that she refused to send his picture in because he had gone over the lines, broken the rules, thought and acted outside the box!

Well, that, as you know, is not allowed. Psychiatrists and psychologists and the government and the great religions of the world all want us to be in little boxes where we will think and act according to their rules.

John Edmondson was deeply hurt and could not understand his mother's reaction when all the time he knew that is was OK to think and act outside the box (or beyond the cross if you are a Christian).

A year later John Edmondson was bundled off to boarding school at the tender age of six.

Chapter Two

School

The box, the box, the box. The box was back. John Edmonson soon learned that life was not going to be easy. Like his beloved mother and like the stupid man who drew that colouring in picture with its lines and rules that were inflexible, he was to find school a never ending continuum of boxes, lines, rules and man-made laws.

Don't think outside the box!
Don't cross the line!
Don't break the rules!

Don't do this, don't do that, don't, don't, don't. What a drag. Why must a six year old tuck his shirt in? Why must he pull up his socks? Why must he eat all his food at night when his hunger had already been satisfied and he could just sense that cook had put too much salt on the meat and too much sugar in the pumpkin and over cooked the cabbage! Why, why, why? But to ask, oh hell no! That was disrespectful to his elders and could result in being sent to bed with no food at all. Only six and already caught in a catch-22 situation. Eat what you know is bad for you or eat nothing at all.

Then there was school itself. Lessons. Learning. Language. Mathematics. Physical Education and much more. Why was it necessary to learn to add numbers in a particular way when he could do it faster another way? The box was back and the teacher bellowed "This is how we do it!"

Why year after year did he have to sit in a class of dimwits where the teacher taught only at the speed of the slowest pupil? No wonder he and some of the other kids were always being punished for being "naughty." They were just simply bored and wanted to get on with it.

Maybe home schooling was the answer but then that just wasn't heard of in the late 1940's in a rural part of South Africa. Yet John Edmondson did read about it when he was sent a book by a great aunt in a far away land for Christmas one year.

When he asked his parents if he could have a governess their answer was simple. Their answer was no. Why not? The government does not allow it. You have to go to a proper school. You have to learn and think the way the government wants you to learn and think. You have to grow up to be a pillar of society. You have to grow up to think and act like a good citizen. In other words you have to toe the line boy. You have to be happy in your little box. Besides which, even if we were allowed to get you a governess we could not afford it and you damn well know it! So that's that. Now eat your porridge and speak when you are spoken to. This happened over the Christmas holidays one year when John Edmondson was about seven. The next day he took a lonely stroll to the riverside where he sat and watched the water trundle by. He was fascinated by the sounds that the water made as it shot over some pebbles or found its way around a larger stone. Sometimes it splashed against the bank and the water seemed to rise a little higher or it swirled and eddied in a pool and moved slower for a while. It did not seem to be boxed in at all and yet John Edmonson knew that its freedom, like his, was also limited. The water could only flow downstream and it seemed to be limited to its left and to its right by what we call riverbanks. These could be broken only in the severest of circumstances. Like a mega storm for example. Then the river could be free to go its own way and find new paths, but alas, these were exceptions and seemed always to end in some kind of disaster.

Why was the water in the river boxed in? Why could it not ever flow upstream? Why was it limited to flowing only within the limits of it's banks? Surely there must be a way beyond the box. Ah, and then he got it, at the tender age of seven John Edmondson got it.

When the water reached the sea and perhaps even before then, some of it would separate and rise into the sky, out of the box! (We call it evaporation – even though it continues to exist). John Edmondson realized that he too, could, like the water, rise out of the box of human humdrum existence. Alas, at this age he did not know how and there was no one to guide him.

Chapter Three

Learning about Life

A new school
.

John Edmondson's dad had moved during the school holidays due to the forest where he was working being mowed down to make some kind of mining props for the gold mines on the reef. It seems that taking things out of the ground is more important to man than putting things into it. The price of gold had been fixed at $28.00 an ounce and in 1949 that was good. It would make the mine magnates rich and the government was happy too, as much of the country's revenue comes from gold mining.

But John Edmondson's dad did not like the government nor did he like the rich owners of the gold mines. He worked on a gold mine once, and said that the owners exploited the workers, paying poorly and forcing the miners to work in dangerous and most unhealthy conditions. Many workers were killed or maimed in mining accidents. John Edmondson visited the reef once with his father. His father pointed out the large mountains of dust and waste that was left when the gold bearing ore had been brought from deep under the earth and crushed and reduced to a fine powder from whence the gold could be extracted and melted down.

Those dirty mountains were not pleasant to be near to on windy days as the wind would blow the fine dust all over the place and really upset the local housewives who could not keep their houses neat and clean and had to close the doors and windows, even on hot and stuffy days, to keep the dust out. Yet this dust was so fine it seemed to get in everywhere. Also it contained a poison which was used in the extraction of the gold and this poison caused plants and fish to die and made many people develop allergies and other ailments.

John Edmondson's dad told him that those mountains were not really mountains of dust but that they were mountains of men: an attribute to all the miners who had lost their lives working underground and a reminder of the greed of the mine owners and the government who appeared to be the sole beneficiaries of this strange activity called gold mining. Of course the rich women who wore expensive gold jewellery were also indirectly to blame, but only to a very small extent because they just liked pretty things and were not the instigators.

So because of this John Edmondson had to go to a new school and that meant new rules and new boxes. He had come to this new school with a report card from his old school and immediately the new school master taunted him: "Oh, a clever one, I see. Well you will have to show us just how clever you are. We all know that the school you went to was a very small one and that Mr. du Toit, your teacher, was very fond of the bottle. Now, Johnny, this is a big school, we have got four teachers here and you will have to toe the line. We have strict rules and you will obey them. No playing in the girls' play ground. We believe in separation here. No playing with the senior boys. You must respect them"… and on and on and on it went. Box, after box, after box.

John Edmondson could feel his love of life just being squeezed out of him as if he were an orange being held by a huge hand and having the juice slowly removed.

Was there no way out of the box?

But there was a way! Slowly John Edmondson recalled how Mr. du Toit at his first school used to open the lessons in the morning with a prayer. He always told them to close their eyes and then he would talk to someone nobody ever saw. He called this person God. It seemed that if you knew this God and if you asked him nicely he could do things for you if you were good and if you obeyed him. But alas! There was the box again. You had to love him with all your heart and soul and you had to obey all his commandments. But how could a seven year old do this if he had not even met this person called God?

At home John Edmondson's parents clearly did not have much time for this God. He worked this out because they never prayed like Mr. du Toit did and they never went to church like Mr. du Toit said all self respecting adults should. So one day John Edmondson said to his mother: "Why don't you go to church?" and his mother replied: " John, we are Presbyterians and there is no Presbyterian church here. The big church in town is a Dutch Reformed church and your father does not understand their language. In the next town there is a Roman Catholic church but we cannot go there. They are too different."

At the tender age of seven, John Edmondson was already learning that the religions of the world do not stand together. Later he would learn that there are over 2000 registered Christian religions spread all over the world. Yet he had heard Mr. du Toit speak to God whom he referred to as The One God. So had he misunderstood Mr. du Toit?

Was there in fact a different God for each religion, or even worse, a different God for each church or worse or better, a different God for each family or individual on earth or was it all the same one God that served all mankind…. or no God at all?

It was more or less at this time that a great new avenue opened up in John Edmondson's life. His mother's brother died. Well, actually he was brutally murdered in a country called Kenya by people called the Mau Mau. It seemed there was some kind of uprising in that land and there was much violence and unrest. But what this meant in John Edmondson's life was that his mother was asked by her late brother's wife if his parents could look after her daughter, who was now fatherless. This question caused much wringing of hands, tears and frustration over the days that followed. John's father was not keen on the idea. As you know he was a very poor man. Reluctantly he conceded to the wishes of John's mother. Thus it came to pass that cousin Charlene arrived by train a while later. She was to stay with the Edmondson's for a year until her mother "sorted things out".

The new school which John Edmondson and his brother were attending was a day school. All the children lived in town and walked to school or like John Edmondson, lived a few miles out of town and were taken there daily by their parents or went by bus or by donkey cart. The donkey cart kids were the most popular because they had a donkey cart driver whose sole duty, as far as John Edmondson could see, was to bring the children to school, wait until school came out and then take them home again. Each day after school a lot of kids would go running after the donkey carts begging for a free ride, jumping on the side, hanging on the back and generally terrorizing the asses. This was clearly a high point of their day but was, of course, not allowed according to school rules. It was forbidden. To overcome this set-back the older boys would take a short cut through the back buildings, the ablution blocks, and waylay the carts where the teachers could not see them!

Back to Charlene and John Edmondson's new experience. Charlene was four years older than John Edmondson and a pretty girl too at the age of eleven. She had reddish hair, a few freckles and was just starting to show the very first signs of womanhood.

Now there was a problem in the Edmondson's house. It was a small house comprising of two bedrooms, a kitchen and a dining room-cum lounge. There was no bathroom. There was a long drop toilet a short distance from the kitchen with the rickety door facing the other way.

For washing there was a basin in the kitchen which was filled with cold water and everyone had a turn at night to wash their hands and faces. A galvanized zinc bathtub was brought in from the lean-to at the rear of the house on a Sunday night and everyone took turns to have a bath. There were no taps and no running water. Water was collected daily in buckets from a nearby well. On a Sunday night it was heated on a coal stove in an old four-gallon paraffin tin. Dad always bathed first and then mom and then big brother. You will note his name is never mentioned in this story. That is because this is John Edmondson's story and he did not get on very well with his big brother. That is an understatement. They disliked each other intensely. To John Edmondson, it seemed from the first day he could remember, that his brother was always teasing and hurting and belittling him in every which way possible. As you have guessed, John Edmondson was always last to bath, and by then the water was usually cold and full of dirty soapy froth which made Sunday nights one of John's less favourite times. Well, things were just about to get a little worse for him. Can you believe it? This little Kenyan cousin was given preference over big brother and John Edmondson when it came to the bathing order. The only consolation that John Edmondson took out of this was that he could stick his tongue out at big brother and say: " Whe, whe, she's bathing before you too!!"

Ah, but the bathing order was only one of the changes that came about. Who would sleep where and with whom? Mother and father had their room with a double bed. Big brother and John Edmondson had their room with two very single beds. By very single is meant the narrowest of single beds that money can buy. These were beds that were just big enough for one teenager to sleep on if he did not toss and turn too much at night.

This raised the question, where was Charlene to sleep? At first she slept with mother and father partly to help her to not be scared in a strange house, partly to help her to come to terms with her grief and partly because there damn well was nowhere else! It soon became apparent, however, that this was not the ideal situation and a solution was required. There was no room in the kitchen or the lounge-cum-dining room for another bed. It would be impossible for any of the children to sleep under the open lean-to at the back of the house. The children's room was too small for three beds. Yet a solution did come. Neighbours, having heard of the Kenyan's plight offered the loan of a somewhat wider bed called a three quarter bed which they felt would be big enough for a seven and eleven year old to share. So for a period of one year it was agreed that these kind people would use John Edmondson's bed for their spare room, which was seldom used, and John Edmondson would share their bed with his cousin Charlene. All well and good. For the first few nights they cuddled up and kept each other warm. Charlene was happy to have a younger "brother" to sleep with and control. It gave her a sense of responsibility!

Novelties wear off. Or do they? For John Edmondson it was going to be one long interesting life of new beginnings. Charlene was a cute cat. The first thing he learned from her was about God and it interested him the most. She taught him how to pray. She taught him that it was possible to escape from the box although she did not really know about being boxed in. Somehow she seemed to be a free spirit although at the time John Edmondson had no conception of what that might be. He just knew, somehow, he just felt that she was different to all the other kids at school. She was freer, happier, more content than the others.

At night as they lay in the dark room broken only by a glint of moonlight and perhaps the flickering of a few stars, they were happy. Big brother seemed to accept the situation at night, yet by day there were clear signs of jealousy. John Edmondson soon accepted that the only real time he could share with Charlene was at night so unless they talked too loudly or giggled too much big brother would ignore them and that suited all three. Thus an acceptance and understanding seemed tacitly to fall into place.

When the moon was new or low the room was very dark as the house was some six miles from town and had no electricity. Neither were there any street lights or even a neighbour's house in sight. Father had one Colman's paraffin lamp and then there was an ordinary paraffin lamp which they used to light up the dinner table at night.

In summer they ate before dark to save on fuel. The children shared one candle in a home made candle stick and it had to be blown out as soon as they were in bed. That meant long, restful but sometimes lonely nights. But with Charlene by his side John Edmondson no longer lay awake during the long hot summer nights. She often told him stories. Oh how he loved to listen to stories. One night she told him the story of Tommy, a little boy who was very sick and this story really touched his tiny heart. It also taught him a new word and a new concept. Tommy was very ill and his mother was praying with him. She was teaching little Tommy a new prayer and it went something like this: "Dear Lord, bless my mommy and my daddy and my brother and my sister. Make me better but should I die before I awake, please Lord my soul to take." What was a soul? John Edmondson had not heard of a soul before. Charlene explained to him that every living body has a soul, a kind of mirror image of the body but made of a substance you cannot see. Unlike the body the soul does not die. So if you believe in God and are good and obey his rules (oh dear, the box is back) he will take your soul or send his angels to fetch your soul and take it to where it can live happily ever after. Well, to John Edmondson at least that part sounded good but what happened if you were naughty? Oh dear. But it was getting late and John Edmondson's eyes could not see in the dark room and his mind was growing hazy as sleep took over.

Except for the fact that there were now more mouths to feed and less to eat, things moved on pretty much as usual in the Edmondson's household. Dad seemed more irritable and there was a tension between him and Mrs Edmondson that was not there before.

Charlene's mother had promised to send money from time to time to help with Charlene's upkeep but by August the only thing that had arrived was a small box of Kenyan tea. What seemed to upset Mr. Edmondson was the hint in Charlene's mom's latest letter that she would be happy if John Edmondson's parents could foster Charlene for another year as things were still bad in Kenya.

There was no way that Mr. Edmondson was going to fall for that one and he made it clear that Charlene would be put on the first train back after school closed in December. Charlene did not seem to mind either way but John Edmondson could see how his mother was hurting. He felt rather bitter towards his dad, but then he did not understand the complexities of income and expenditure yet.

Chapter Four

On the move

On the move again.

Ever seen the picture of the people moving and the ghosts moving with them? Well, that's how John felt at the age of ten when his father was on the move again and so too were the rest of the family including the dogs and the fowls.

At the age of ten John is old enough to tell his own story. He is irritable and he tells it his way. In short, he cuts the crap. So here goes……..

A long and painful journey in a five ton International truck, open at the back with the meagre furniture tied with rope but not covered.

There was much damage done to the furniture on the trip due to the elements: wind and dust and later a shower of rain. The poor condition of the corrugated gravel roads did not help either. The driver, my mother, myself and my brother all squashed in the front of the cab. My father, seeking shelter between the furniture, on the back of the truck.

After almost a full day's travel we arrived at a strange house. We were told to wait while my father made enquiries within. This was not the house in which we were to live. It was the house of my father's fellow worker. We were invited to sit under a tree on a patch of grass. Sometime later three young boys joined us but they did not speak our language. We were served cold tea and dry biscuits. My brother would not eat or drink as he complained of a headache (which he was to me before and has been to me ever since). The oldest of the three boys we had just met tried to make conversation. My brother just said his head was sore. I did not speak because I was shy. Also I could not speak their language very well.

Sometime later my father emerged and we set off again. As the sun was setting on the flat plains of the highveld we arrived at our "new" home. The dogs were let loose. The fowls were off-loaded and given crushed mealies and water but kept in their hocks. Unloading began as the sun started to set. Fortunately it was summer and the day was hot. We began carrying in what furniture we had, piece by piece, into a ramshackled house, where we were to live for the next three years.

To me this house seemed like a palace. It was my first experience of a stone and mud home. Until now we had always lived in makeshift galvanized iron shacks. As in the past, this house had no running water and no electric power. The nearest water was some hundred yards away in a dirty well. At night we relied on one paraffin lamp to light the kitchen which became our main living area.(The other paraffin lamp had been broken during the move). It was in the kitchen that we cooked, ate and bathed. The house had no bathroom. To go to bed my brother and I were allowed the use of a candle, but only on dark nights if the moon did not supply sufficient light. The latrine was a long drop about thirty metres away from the house, with a path which had been walked to it through the long, long grass.

After settling in it was time to move on with our lives. Dad set off to the forest which he was to denude for the benefit of the gold mining industry. Mom carried on with her daily chores of cooking, washing, ironing, feeding the fowls and so forth. Soon it was time for brother and me to go to our new school.

We were now living in the first period of the new Afrikaner nationalist government in South Africa. These people were determined to stamp their narrow minded biblical based authority on the nation. If you were not one of them, then there was little place for you. Being a very small English minority in a large Afrikaans speaking controlled school, we were soon ostrasized and pushed into a separate classroom. We were treated almost like the untouchables in India. If the treatment we received seemed harsh, imagine the lot of the black people who were treated with absolute disdain, who were considered as slaves rather than people of value. It was while we were at this school that the government was re-elected to its second term of office and really started to show its ugly teeth. It was here that the idea of separatism became official government policy and was soon to be known throughout the whole world by the detestable term of 'apartheid'.

But let my story not be detoured by the politics of the day. Suffice to say that I had more time to think and to question God. How could a reasonable, a loving, a fair God allow such injustice amongst his children? The ministers of religion were telling us not to question authority but to go with the flow or we would be hurt. This seemed cruel and unrealistic to my mind and I needed to find a way out of the box. Once more I knew that I, John Edmondson, was boxed in by society, by religion and by what appeared to be the thinking pattern of the ruling party. Even at the tender age of ten, eleven and twelve, which I was during the three years of desolation on the bare and windswept highveld region where we were now staying, I knew something was not right. But these years brought no answers.

Chapter Five

A new era.

A new era of confrontation and misunderstanding was about to start. Once more my father's work took us to another part of the country. By this time the new government was feeling strong and flexing its muscles. English speaking children were now totally banned from attending Afrikaans schools – not to mention our black brothers who were basically banned from attending any school whatsoever. More about that later… maybe…

Having arrived at our new destination and for the first time to live in a town - not way out in or close to, a forest - new challenges were to be faced. I was due to attend high school and I was being forced to go to an English speaking school against my wishes. Remember that I had attended Afrikaans schools since day one. This meant that except for the mother tongue usage at home, my natural or adopted language and my thinking pattern, language wise of course, had become that of the Afrikaner.

I begged and pleaded to be allowed to attend the local Afrikaans school but I was simply told that this was against government policy. No longer would English speaking children be allowed at their schools as we would contaminate the purity of their nation. School leaving English speaking kids could also no longer get jobs in the civil service or any government related institution. This seemed unfair to me, but no doubt was a simple repetition that was taking place in different parts of this planet, and no doubt would repeat itself again in the future, as one group of people gained power over another. Funnily enough, it was this experience that allowed me out of the box for the first time and for just a little while. It was this experience and an article which I read in a daily paper about an unidentified flying object that set my mind racing. Was it possible that there was intelligent life out there? Out where? Out there far away! Of course this whole idea was pooh-poohed by the intelligentsia of the time and definitely condemned in the strongest manner by the religious leaders. Yet it played on my mind. On and on and round and round it went in my mind. "Windmills of my mind". I'm certain that you have heard the song. Surely, I thought, there must be life beyond this little planet of ours. Why would God choose this one big rock to place intelligent life on? Surely, I reasoned, even with the knowledge available to man in 1955, there had to be bigger, better and more advanced planets capable of sustaining life. So what made Earth special? But no, I was getting out of the box and that was not allowed. One could not raise such questions. One could not write such things even in a school essay without being chastised privately and taunted in front of the whole class for having such "ridiculous" ideas.

Then a new thing struck. Well it was new in my life anyway. A polio epidemic swept the nation and everyone had to be vaccinated. All sport and physical recreational activities had to be stopped forthwith and until further notice due to the fact that physical exercise was thought to encourage the polio virus which left a number of my fellow scholars crippled for life. Well, I thought again but was afraid to say, "Is this the eternal loving God that is punishing our people for bad behaviour?" Maybe it was. Maybe it wasn't. I was in the box and I was not allowed to question my maker or my superiors. I thought that the reason that they did not allow me to question them was that they did not know themselves. In fact, I was damn sure that they did not know. And here it was that I started to realize "hey man, I have a brain. I can think. I don't have to just do what I am told to do. I don't have to just believe what I am told to believe. I CAN THINK! I can figure things out for myself." This was rather scary because it opened up a new dimension. It was to lead, not to utopia or any major discovery that would change the world for the better. However, it would clarify certain misunderstandings about a great faith, a foolish faith, a faith dare I say it, clung to and blindly followed by millions of earth beings. More of that later.

It was really difficult being expected to understand the niceties of English grammar when one had not been taught the basics of this great language. It was no wonder that at the end of my first term at an English school I did exceedingly well in all subjects except English. It was to take many years of forced study, and the discipline of putting myself through university to major in English, to overcome this void in my life. (I still make stupid grammatical mistakes as you have no doubt noticed but if 51% of you are prepared to forgive me then I am prepared to live with it). It is strange how many of us feel so inadequate by a perceived weakness that we will go to great measures to turn those very weaknesses into strengths. It was many years later that I was to discover the reason for this. It is part of the DNA structure of mankind embedded in us by our creators…. who came from a distant galaxy. (More of that in another book).

Not only was I experiencing high school for the first time, but a number of other issues were new too. For the first time in my life I was part of an English speaking community. Being at high school there were also new subjects to be learnt. There was algebra, geometry and trigonometry. There was physical science and chemistry. There was Latin and bookkeeping. Then there was the idea of being in a boys only school. A different kind of segregation! Most of the kids at this school were boarders coming from far away cities. They were the children of the well-to-do upper class. Once again I found myself in a unique minority. I was part of a small group of day scholars from the local town. We were all lower class and poor. My parents were undoubtedly of the very poorest. So once again I found myself looked down upon. We could not afford the school uniform. Fortunately the head master was in his final year before retirement and couldn't care too much about how we dressed.

The next year saw major changes. The new head master, an ex-pupil, was determined to "restore" the school to its former glory. This meant that every boy was to dress perfectly like an English gentlemen. Full school uniform including straw hats was enforced. This meant unaffordable expenses for my parents. My mother was forced to go to work for the first time in her married life. This brought new hardship to our family. It meant that I was left to my own devices in the afternoons. (Big brother had left home to do compulsory military service…my dad said it would make a man out of him…my mother wept silently and I was more than half delighted to see him go and hoped that that was that). I had to make my own lunch. I had to light the fire at four o'clock in the afternoon. Although we now had some electricity in the house, it was for lights only. A stove that used wood for cooking and heating was still the main source of energy.

Although we now had running water, it still had to be heated by means of the stove and would only stay warm for a short while after the fire ceased to burn.

Due to the fact that we lived some five miles (that is eight kilometres in the metric system) from the school it was impossible for me to partake in extra mural activities. Although I yearned to play cricket with the other boys, it was not possible. There were two reasons for this. Firstly the matches lasted from three to six o'clock in the afternoons. How could I play cricket and make the fire at the same time? Secondly we could not afford the cricket uniform required. So once again I found myself on the outside looking in. But this was not altogether a bad thing. You see, it allowed me, temporarily, at any rate, to get out of the box. Had I been able to conform to all the school requirements without difficulty I truly would have been boxed in without even knowing it. You see, we humans have a tendency to want to conform. We want to be part of the group. We want to be accepted. Our natural instinct is to go with the flow. This was built into our genes by those who created our DNA structure.

If you go back in history you will see that all the great changes that took place were brought about by people who managed to get out of the box. These were the people who saw things differently. These were the people who acted otherwise. These were the revolutionaries.

On the one hand I sorely wanted to conform and be part of the group. On the other hand one little molecule in my DNA seemed to be out of place. Psychologists ask the question: "Are we controlled by our environment or by our genes?" It seems to me that it is a bit of both. At the end of the day however, it seems that the overriding factor is the genes.

Let us not labour the high school days. They passed with little of note. The end came. I was honoured with a bursary for exceptional achievement over the full five years of my stay at high school. This was not sufficient to send me to university although I had now become obsessed with the idea of further education.

My father said I should get a nice comfortable job in the civil service. You see, he said, civil servants do very little work. They have nice cozy offices, medical aid, sick leave, annual leave and a comfortable pension to look forward to.

Alas, my efforts to become a civil servant were in vain. You see, I had become an Englishman and with a surname like mine I had no chance of getting into the civil service of the day. A damn good thing too, in retrospect. You see, had I became a civil servant the lid of my box would have been closed forever and I would have died just another number. I would have been buried in just another row in just another cemetery.

But that one out-of-place molecule in my DNA structure kept bugging me to make a difference. All the difference, as you will later see, would be to influence the way in which the majority of people may re-think preconceived boxed ideas. A stimulus in fact to the thinking pattern of the average man. (Unfortunately as you and I know, the average man is not a thinker. In fact he is not even a doer, nor a reader and most of the time not even a listener. So, full marks to you, my friend. If you have read this far you are not the proverbial average man. But your real challenge will come later. Keep an open mind!)

My father's second choice for me was thus to join the commercial world and earn a living. He was not one for learning and he played down my dreams for tertiary education.

Before any thoughts of earning a living, however, there was another big question to be faced. Military service! All young able bodied white men were expected – no, not expected – forced to do military service. The options at the time were three months of hard drill, followed by a two week call up for ten consecutive years, or, for a small number of lucky young men there was the alternative of completing one's military service in a solid stretch of one year. There was one final option, which allowed one to avoid service. That was to become a religious objector. Basically that meant being or becoming a Jehovah's Witness. As a Jehovah's Witness one may not partake in military service. Unfortunately this meant being placed in the detention barracks for three months. The idea of being isolated and punished in this way did not appeal to me, nor did the idea of joining a particular faith merely to get out of military service.

There was no alternative. It was military service for me. The fact that I had done well at high school helped me to get into the air force on the once off one year plan. That was to me the least objectionable of the options available.

Chapter 6

You're in the army now

A year in the forces.

This was going to be too much. Having heard of all the horrible things that young recruits are put through I was most apprehensive. To be honest, I was downright scared and not looking forward to it one bit. The only up-side to the whole affair was that I had been accepted into the Air Force. As previously stated the norm at the time was to do a three month stint in the army followed by ten years of two week call-ups for ten years thereafter. As this seemed like a real pain in the butt to me, and at the age of 18 a never ending story, I decided to apply for a position in the air force where one could do a year at a single stretch and then be exempt from further peace time call ups. Another option was the navy where a similar one-year option was available to a small number of youngsters.

The navy did not appeal to me, as my father had been in the Royal Navy during the first world war and his experience did nothing to enhance the navy in my eyes. I did not like the idea of being seasick or of floating around in the middle of nowhere for weeks on end with no land in sight. Rough seas scared me and stories of sunken ships and many drownings made me shiver. Nor did the often funny but more often tragic stories of drunken sailors appeal to me. My parents were both teetotallers and I found the very thought of drinking alcohol abhorrent. Little did I know that I would later become addicted to the stuff. Anyhow, I had made it into the air force and maybe I would be one of the lucky 20 out of 800 intakes for the year that would be chosen to be trained as a pilot.

Every Air Force recruit wanted to be a pilot. So did I.

The first 3 months of training were very rough. It was basic military training. When they say basic military training they mean basic. Very basic. Attention! Forward march! Left right, left right! Fortunately that was only from 7am to 5:30pm Mondays to Fridays and Saturday mornings 7am to 1pm or as they like to say in the forces seven hundred hours until thirteen hundred hours. Well, it wasn't just marching. There was plenty of punishment in between as well. Halt!

The corporal in charge shouted: "Halt, John – you are out of step. Do you see that tree over there (about a mile away) – go and fetch me a leaf from it and hurry up – on the double!" Back with a leaf fifteen minutes later and the corporal shouts: "Not that leaf, idiot! Now go and put it back and bring me the one above it and this time HURRY UP!"

It was not all hardship though, let's be fair. We did get breakfast of porridge and milk early in the mornings after standing in a queue for a long time. As there were 800 of us the sergeant major in charge was kind enough to arrange two queues so that meant you would only have 399 other recruits in front of you if you were a little late. We also had an hour for lunch served in tin plates. This was usually a few slices of really thick bread with soup (summer and winter) and hot tea. Suppertime it was the same story. Here the food varied somewhat and we came to look forward to Fridays when it was fish and chips.

After about a month of this routine we were starting to get fit and the fat boys were looking more like men. This obviously worried the authorities and suddenly the tea took on a bluish colour and tasted a bit funny. The thirsty guys drank it but soon the news spread. "The tea is loaded with blue vitriol." That is copper sulphate! Now we soon learned that this was meant to kill a man's natural instincts. This meant NO TEA or be happy with just a piece of string hanging between your legs.

Now I think it is generally known that young men are a virile lot. Most of us were in the 18-20 year old age group. As we were not allowed out of camp for the first 3 months this presented a problem. Day visitors were also not allowed and night visitors absolutely not. So, how now, brown cow? There were a few young men who doubled up as AC-DC's but this was not the norm. Also in the year 1960 the word "gay" was not yet used in conservative South Africa and there were no gay rights. So how do close on 800 young men satisfy their natural instincts? Needless to say self-satisfaction was the order of the day. Yet there were those who would not be denied the real thing. This is where the bush telegraph came in to play. Also use of the one and only public telephone. With the use of long tickeys free calls could be made to the local house of disrepute and arrangements made for "gang bangs" at a greatly reduced price and at a special "safe" venue. Now, the question remained as to how to get out of the secure camp. Well, not to put a spoke in the wheel of today's young recruits all over the world, I shall refrain from telling you how and where the young soldiers and the ladies of the night coupled. The fact of the matter is they did.

Slowly I thought I was getting out of the box. I certainly was learning some new tricks. The ladies of the night were experienced in the pleasures of the flesh and for a small fee were more than willing to satisfy many an eager young man who invariably shot his bolt in no time at all. NEXT!

Enough of that. The long tickeys mentioned earlier fascinated me. It was from fellow recruits that I learned just how easy it was to make even long distance telephone calls from a public telephone booth absolutely free of charge. In 1960 we still used the British monetary system of the day. Public telephones required that you put a tickey (two and a half cents) into a slot. (South Africa changed to a decimal system in 1962 shortly after the Union of South Africa broke ties with the British and became a Republic). Anyhow, the phones were still operated via a manual exchange and when the operator told the caller how much to deposit in the slot one simply let the relevant coin drop into the slot the number of times needed! You see it was attached by a long piece of strong cotton or thin fishing gut by means of a sliver of chewing gum. The same coin could thus be used over and over again. Of course this was strictly illegal and although we were threatened with all kinds of punishment should we be caught, no one ever was.

The three months basic training came to an end as all things do. At last it was time for the men to be sorted from the boys. It was time for the selection of the trainee pilots to take place. There was much excitement as we were called for testing. Not everyone was given the opportunity though. There were those who did not qualify on the grounds of their education and there were those who were colour blind. The rest of us underwent a very strict series of tests.

First there were the physical tests. Then there were extreme hearing and eyesight tests. Then there were innumerable aptitude tests. After two weeks of continuous intensive testing all but twenty young recruits would have their dreams dashed with the question: "Sorry - what was your second choice? Or your third choice? Your fourth choice?" Not surprisingly but very disappointingly I was not chosen to be a pilot. This was a big blow to my ego and the first of many in my adult life. Not only was I not selected to be trained as a pilot but my second choice also went down the drain. I really thought I was good enough to be a navigator, but was told that you needed an A for mathematics to make it as a navigator and I had only a B minus. Oh well, third choice then – radar operator. "Good luck, well done!" So that was that then. Who cares? Another nine months of hell and it will all be over. "This too shall pass."

Then a glimmer of hope. How terribly cruel young men can be. We heard that one of the trainee pilots had been killed in a crash on his first solo flight. What did we do? Did we go to his funeral? No. We stood in line and volunteered to take his place. One candidate was chosen. As for the rest of us it was back to the salt mines.

What never ceased to amaze me was the small-mindedness of the force. From the top brass down to the lowest private. It is generally known that if the commander-in-chief of any division wakes up in a bad mood or nicks himself shaving the whole division will suffer that day. The saying goes that he will take it out on his subordinate who will shout at his subordinate, who will swear at the Sergeant-Major who will punish the next man down and so on. The lowest ranked lance corporal gives the privates extra drill. It is said that all the poor old private can do is to kick the cat. But there was no cat. So what happened? At the end of a long day we turned on each other and this inevitably led to a bloody nose or two.

The basic training over and the twenty trainee pilots chosen, and the twenty trainee navigators chosen there wasn't much for the remaining 760 (minus one for the poor fellow who crashed) recruits to do. We learnt what we had to learn and did what we had to do. We still did a fair amount of basic drill every day and after six months most of us were ultra fit. We were now allowed the odd weekend pass. A weekend meant Saturday from 1pm until Sunday 11pm. It was at this stage that boredom started to set in and the brighter boys got itchy feet.

We discovered that we could buy our way out of the force for a relatively small sum of money. A "small sum" being about one and a half month's salary. A "small sum" to the rich kids was in fact a "small fortune" to me and so the idea played on my mind for only a short while. You see, there was a down side to buying your freedom. The down side was that you then were liable for normal army call up and to avoid that was one of the reasons why we had volunteered for the twelve month stint in the first place. Thus after contemplating buying myself out of this particular box, I soon realized the folly of the idea and also saw that it would not set me free but merely place me in a bigger box.

I have been asked: "what does a radar operator do?" Well in 1960 it was a pretty routine and exceedingly boring job. I cannot say too much because we were sworn to secrecy and put under the threat of death if we divulged any state secrets. The fact is there were no real secrets and the job of a radar operator was simply one of sitting in a mobile unit watching little blips on a screen for four-hour shifts twice a day. One tracked these little blips (specks of light) across the screen and worked out their speed, height, etc. These specks were really aircraft in the sky and our main duty was to watch for "enemy" aircraft, which thankfully were never seen during our training period.

The months passed and eventually the time came for our final parade – the passing out parade, our year was over.

Chapter Seven

Banking

Military service a thing of the past. Nineteen years old. My father said to me "The world is your oyster." Having never been to the sea-side I had never seen an oyster. I also must have missed that saying at school so I did not really know what it meant. The way my father said it made me feel that it was good. It is interesting how much importance one places on how things are said rather than what is actually said. Often meaning is conveyed not so much by what is said but by how it is said. I had heard that pearls grow in oysters and I knew that a pearl was not only a thing of beauty but that a good pearl was valuable too. I read John Steinbeck's book "The Pearl" and learned from it that if you set your heart on something it was worth forsaking all else to achieve your dream. Yet there was something that I did not like about oysters. They clammed so tightly shut that one had to prize them open with great effort. This often resulted in the extremely hard shell being damaged and pieces of grit entering the slimy meat of the oyster. I could not believe that people actually ate these things. The real reason that I did not like oysters though was that they reminded me of the box – almost impossible to open! Would I ever find a way out?

No more uniform to hide behind. I had to find work. I had to pay my way. So I figured that what my father really said to me was. "Move your backside and find a job. We have looked after you for long enough." Since it was nigh impossible for an Englishman to get a "safe" job in the civil service the next best thing seemed to be the banking business. This too was rather straight laced but seemed the most reasonable alternative at the time. My father had had a hard life in the private sector and seemed determined to steer me into something more comfortable. Either state or state like, I guess.

Being a very confident young man and having scored highly in Bookkeeping and Accountancy at school I took it for granted that my application at one of the town's leading banks would be received favourably. It was. I started my first real job less than two weeks later. Having a natural flair for figures I took to banking like a duck to water. I enjoyed the work and made rapid progress. By the end of two years I was already in a middle management position. In retrospect I should have made a career out of banking. I reckon that I would have done very well for myself. One is generally wiser after the event. One really valuable lesson that I learnt in the bank was the value of money and how to make it grow. It is imperative for anyone who wishes to accumulate wealth during his lifetime to follow a few basic principles. The first is to spend less than you earn. The second is to invest your savings in an interest bearing account. The third is not to spend your savings or the interest on your savings. Both the savings and the interest on your savings must be allowed to grow. The process may be slow but it is guaranteed and it is exponential. Another step to riches is the acquisition of fixed property, preferably on the outskirts of a growing town or city. I will not go into the intricacies of the stock market here. The only advice I will give is not to take advice from the so-called experts. It is easy for them to manipulate the market by advising their clients to buy shares in a company that is not doing well and of which they themselves hold a fair number of shares. Once enough of their clients jump in, follow their advice and buy thousands of shares the price goes up. The expert then sells his shares and in due course you find yourself worse off than you started. I was learning to make money. Although I enjoyed watching my bank balance grow there was an emptiness in me.

Less than two years after entering the bank I was looking for greener pastures. The bank was good to me and I met some really genuine people there. The senior staff were very helpful and I knew they were grooming me for further promotion. I was always one of the first to arrive in the mornings and one of the last to leave at the end of the day. I enjoyed the structured nature of the work. There were strict guidelines for everything. Although I liked this there was part of me that rebelled. There was that one out of place molecule in my DNA that screamed at me saying: "they are busy sealing the box that you are in! Wiggle your way out or forever remain in the box. It might be comfortable but is that what you want?" It was not what I wanted. I knew that I had to get out while I could still see the light.

As a schoolboy I had dreamed of going to university but knew that my parents could not afford it. I still held tight to this dream and now the idea of being a full time student became an obsession. It seemed that the freedom of thought and the time to ponder on the reason for being would set me free. Questions kept coming up in my mind. I needed answers. Who are we? Where do we come from? Why are we here?

In an effort to find out, I attended many churches who all claimed to have the answers. They did not satisfy me. I read many books on philosophy and religion. I studied firstly the Christian religion which was the logical starting point. Logical because I grew up in what was basically a Christian community. Logical because my parents were Christians even though they did not attend church.

The Methodist church on Sunday. Two, three, four Sundays in a row.

The bible. My mother, bless her soul, had an old King James version which she kept at her bedside. I took this and read it from cover to cover. A very controversial book. Never have I read anything that is so contradictory and full of promises. Claims that this is the most widely read book in the world never ceases to amaze me. Yes, there is a great deal of truth in it and yes, it is full of good guidelines for a positive lifestyle. Generally it gives good advice on health matters; even on money matters…see the parable of the talents. Truly a remarkable book in many ways. It probably was perfect for its time and in its original form. But oh for the follies and greed of man. The Roman Catholic priests got hold of it and well… more of that later.

Anyhow, back to the search for truth, The Dutch Reformed church. The Old Apostolic church. The Apostolic Faith Mission. The Seventh Day Adventists. The Mormons. The Jehovah's Witnesses. The Pentecostals. Over the next ten years I spent a lot of time attending lots of different denominations and asking lots of questions. The closest that I came to the truth that I was searching for came from the spiritualists. They claim that they appeal to reason rather than to faith and that makes sense to me. Unfortunately many charlatans and would-be mediums have penetrated their ranks and this makes them no more credible than the main- stream churches.

During this decade I did a lot of reading. Most of my reading was in search of answers to the unanswerable. I read books on Buddhism, Hinduism, Taoism and many other beliefs. I read the Koran. All the great faiths, I found, had certain things in common. They all believed in a god or gods of high authority. The Jews believe in one god. The Christians have the father, the son and the holy ghost. The Buddhists have the light. The American Indians and many African cultures have the spirits of their forefathers. In more than one religion I found reference to the great flood, to the lost continent of Atlantis and prophecies of Armageddon.

My search for the truth led me to many places. I desperately needed to get out of the box. Maybe university was the answer. But let me not get carried away.

After two years of disciplined banking I resigned. One of my much respected senior accountants gave me good parting advice. He said: "Go all out to achieve you goals in life. Remember though to do all things in moderation." He was 38 years old at the time. He died three years later of a heart attack brought about by eating too much fatty red meat, drinking too much red wine and smoking too many unfiltered cigarettes.

Chapter Eight

University

Freedom.
Boxless.
Happiness.
Joy.
Penniless.
Oh dear!

The joy of freedom.
Free to think.
Free to do.

At last I was doing something that I really and truly wanted to do. I was exploring the reason for living.

You may well ask how I could afford to go off to study for four years with paupers as parents and almost nothing in the bank myself. Where there is a will there is a way. I wanted to study. My good marks at school allowed me to apply for a bursary through the Department of Education. My application was approved. There were a number of catches though:

1. Tuition only would be paid for by the department
2. Books and other study material was not covered
3. Board and lodging was not covered
4. I had to sign a contract with the department agreeing to teach at one of the government schools for a period of not less than three years immediately after completing my degree. If I failed to do so I would have to repay the department the bursary, which would then be seen as an interest bearing loan.

Never mind points two, three and four. The only one that mattered at this stage was number one.
I had been accepted and I was to receive free tuition. Varsity here I come!

It did not take long for disenchantment to set in. It did not take long for me to discover that what I saw as my way to free thinking was in fact just the way in to another very big box. To make matters worse there were many boxes within this box and even boxes within those boxes. Society seemed determined to put people into boxes, tie them up and label them clearly. Some people put themselves in boxes and seemed happy to do so.

There was the arts box.
There was the commerce box.
There was the science box.
There was the engineering box.

The fact that the professors referred to them as faculties did not fool me. They were boxes. Within the arts box there was the box for drama, the box for music, the box for literature, boxes for foreign languages. The latter contained boxes of its own. The box for European languages. The box for African languages. The box for Oriental languages. There were further divisions (or smaller boxes) within these boxes. Within the Oriental languages there was Chinese, Indian and Japanese and each of these had dialects for smaller boxes. This was true for the other faculties as well. The engineers were divided into chemical engineers, physical engineers, civil engineers and who knows what else. Divide and rule. That's what it was.

Besides the faculty boxes there were the boxes that the students created for themselves. There was the first year box, the second year box, the third year box, the post graduate box and so on. Then there were the professors, the senior lectures, the junior lectures and more. Oh and then of course the students loved the accommodation boxes. There were a number of hostels and each had a unique box of its own. Here, alas, I was one of the small minority again. As I could not afford to live in a hostel I was a day student. I found a small room not too far from the varsity in the back yard of a little old lady's house. It was actually the servant's room but as the little old lady could not afford a servant she let me stay there rent-free in return for mowing the lawn and tending the garden.

Having chosen my subjects of study for the first year I had to acquire the necessary study material. New textbooks were very expensive. There were alternatives though. There was a second hand bookshop where you could buy books at about one quarter of the original price. Then there was the library where you could sit down and do as much research as you wished. The only drawback here was time. The library closed at eight pm Mondays to Fridays and at one pm on Saturdays and did not open on Sundays. Another drawback was that some other poor student was already busy with the book that you needed when you arrived there. Of course one could always borrow a text book from a rich kid but this too was not always easy as they had after all, bought them to use themselves and inevitably needed them at the same time as you did. So yet another way was found: group study. The bookless would link up with one or more book owners and work together on a project. The rich book owners did the least work while the bookless did not mind putting in the extra effort. So by these various ways of learning I managed my studies at minimal pain to my pocket.

I took my studies very seriously. The subject I enjoyed most was psychology. It gave me some insight into the strange behaviour of mankind. I also enjoyed environmental studies and realized just how rapidly man was messing up the world. Unfortunately these were not subjects taught at school. Since I was studying on a government bursary I had to choose two subjects taught in government schools and at secondary level as my majors. For the rest they did not seem to mind. So I ended up with English and Mathematics as my majors. Not a perfect combination but the subjects with the biggest teacher shortage at the time. The authorities assured me that this combination would always ensure me a job in the teaching profession. For the rest I was free to study what I wanted.

I found it difficult adapting to a student's life after having been in the forces for a year and in the bank for two years prior. Also, I was three years older than most of the other first year students due to the fact that most of them came straight from school. Being a day student as opposed to a resident meant I was on the outside looking in when it came to socializing. Most of the social activities were organized within the residences. When it came to dating I had an advantage. Being older and "wiser" than the girls in my different classes, I had an edge. Most of the first year girls preferred dating second or third year students. Perhaps my "maturity" appealed to them. The fact is I had no problem with dates. Had I not been relatively shy at that stage of my life I could have played the field. As it turned out I settled for a redhead and we had a good steady relationship that lasted the best part of two years.

Then I met the most beautiful woman I had ever seen. I say *had* because if I were to say *have* I may not be allowed to finish this story. (My wife occasionally has a peek at my writing). Anyhow, about this beautiful woman. Everything about her yelled stay away! She was four years older than me. She was German. She was a divorcee. She had three children. She was dating the senior English lecturer. I was drawn to her like a moth to a flame. I was putty in her hands. Suddenly nothing that had gone before mattered. Miracle of miracles. She liked me. The senior English lecturer did not. I never dreamed that such a beautiful woman would ever look in my direction. Yet soon we were dating. She was marvelous company. She was so intelligent. Streets ahead of all the students I had met. Worldly wise too. It did not occur to me at the time, but being four years my senior and the mother of three she must have known a thing or two about life. What followed was probably the most exhilarating two years ever. It was sad that my English marks took a serious turn for the worse at this stage. I wonder why? It did not matter. I was ecstatically happy. She confessed her love for me and at times our conversation even touched on the possibility of a future together. Even her children liked me. Heaven had arrived. For a while I didn't even care about the box. I don't think I even knew that it existed. She was all I needed. She was all I wanted. Life was complete. Oral contraceptives were not yet the order of the day. Abortions were illegal. Abstinence was impossible. What will be will be.

Time went by. At the end of my third year I graduated. Then a year at teachers' training college to complete my tertiary education. The year went by like a dream. Berthildt and I were complete in each other.

Now came the time for us to part. It is said that some people come into your life for a reason, some for a season but only one or two for a lifetime. Berthildt's season had come and gone. It had been a good season. It had been a very good season. The finality of our last goodbye was irrevocable. She went her way. I went mine. We never made contact again.

What caused my beautiful Berthildt and me to separate? Did I want the separation? No. Did she want the separation? No. Sometimes the intellect overrules the heart. She was clever. Very clever. I was above average. Between the two of us we considered ourselves to be pretty intellectual. Maybe that was stupid. We sat down over a cup of coffee and cold-bloodedly decided to go our separate ways for financial reasons. She had a contract to teach in German South West Africa (now Namibia) and I was contracted to teach in the old Transvaal (now Gauteng, Limpopo and North West Province). If either of us broke our contract we would have been in serious debt. Had we followed our hearts and married it would have spelt serious financial difficulties for a long time to come. Remember she had three children all at school by then. So we bit our lips, burnt our bridges and went our separate ways. We were sure that any attempt to keep the flame burning would have eaten holes in our hearts. The future is not ours to see.

During my years as a student I had time to go to many churches. I had time to study many religions. I had time to look into Greek mythology. I even learned about the ancient Anglo Saxon Druids and much more. Still I was no closer to the truth than the day I had started. In the Book of Revelation we read about a scroll sealed with seven seals. The lamb himself opens the seals. How many seals on my box, I wondered? Would someone, someday, open them for me?

Chapter Nine

Teaching

Have university degree.
Have teaching diploma
Will teach.

What started as a quest for intellectual freedom a few years earlier rapidly turned into a huge bottomless pit of quicksand.

I found myself teaching the senior classes in a rough mining community. To add to my woes I was made a housemaster in the boys hostel.

What did I teach? Mathematics, mathematics, mathematics. From Monday 8am until Friday 2pm. Up, shaven and fully dressed at 5.30am every morning in order to see that the boys responded to my ringing the bell at six. Breakfast was at seven. Lunch at 2.30pm, supper at 7pm. I had to say grace at all meals.

The headmaster was a tyrant. "Hitler reincarnated", the other teachers said. Immediately after lunch followed supervised homework and then compulsory sport. For the boys this meant rugby in winter and cricket in summer. Of course it had to be supervised by a teacher. Now although the 800 pupils consisted of pretty close on 400 boys and 400 girls, when it came to the teaching staff the ladies outnumbered the men five to one. So as far as sport and discipline was concerned you can see that the male teachers were grossly overloaded.

After supervising sport until just before supper it was supper followed by compulsory study until 9.15pm. This was followed by half an hour of free time for the boys.

These youngsters, aged from thirteen to eighteen were allowed half an hour of free time before lights out at exactly 9.45pm. No free time for the housemasters though. We were expected to patrol the corridors and maintain discipline. There were four of us and we had to control close on four hundred unruly boys.

Weekends were not too bad. In winter the master's duty was to referee one rugby game every Saturday. If it was an away game it also meant driving the school bus to and from the other school. This could be as much as a two-hour drive. In summer, Saturday offered no free time at all. Cricket lasted from nine in the morning until six in the evening and the headmaster insisted that the housemaster umpire the game. This was in the interest of fair play, of course!

Sundays? This was where I went off religion for the first time. I had to march all the children, boys and girls, to church. There was a very big Methodist church about a mile from the hostel and the children had to wear their school uniform. The preacher was a sour old sod. If he put me off religion imagine what he did to all those poor children.

It was a sad thing that the headmaster had only the results of his matriculants at heart. I suppose that is important. Yet I wondered "should we not be teaching these children what to do with what they were learning rather than simply preparing them to pass an exam?"

By the end of the third of the four school terms in my first year of teaching, I had had enough of the Fuehrer. I had been offered a post at another school but the Fuehrer refused to let me go. I do not know what the rule is now, but in those days the headmaster had the final say. When I told him that if he did not let me go I would resign from the teaching profession, he bellowed: "I will not let you hold a gun to my head!" I lost my rag and gave a term's notice. I was not going to give up without a fight though. I made an appointment with and went to see a very senior member of the Department of Education in the capital city. This was some three hours drive from the school where I was stationed. I had met this man a number of times in my final year as a student and I was sure he would come to my rescue. He did not. Thus ended my non-illustrious career as a teacher!

When I arrived back at school after taking a day's "leave", I found the smug little headmaster waiting for me. He had been informed of my visit by the man I had been to see. The rest of my days at that school were not easy. But I did not let the Fuehrer have it all his own way though. On one occasion I openly refused to cane the boys when he decided that all the boys were to be put through six of the best in front of the girls. I smiled as he turned red and almost had a stroke. I could hear the girls sniggering. This made me smile the more and turned him the redder. Eventually he grabbed the cane out of my hand and proceeded to do the beating himself.

The year of teaching showed me to what extent one man could abuse the power of authority placed in him. I vowed never to do likewise. I swore that whenever I was placed in a position of authority over others I would rule only through the power of respect and never through the power of position.

The last day of my teaching career arrived in due course. It had been a long year. It had been a hard year. I was one year older but two or three years wiser.

Chapter Ten

The pharmaceutical industry.

My mother said to me "Don't worry, when one door closes another door opens." She was a wise old bird, my mom.

It took me less than a month to find work. After a six week training period I was a medical representative. This promised to be good fun. It was also rewarding. The pay was better than that of a teacher. A company car with all expenses paid was included. There was ample free time so I was able to work on getting out of the box again. There was much traveling to do. I got to go to places and to see things I had only dreamed of before. I got to hobnob with the professionals. My clients were medical doctors and pharmacists. I was moving in intellectual circles. It was a mental challenge and I was up to it. Life was great! There were overseas conferences to attend. Beautiful girls were everywhere. It was fun to chat up the doctor's receptionists. Then there were some really attractive female representatives promoting not only medicine but a whole range of interesting products. I remember one particular lass who represented a winery. The boot of her car was always packed full of the latest wines that she was promoting. Needless to say we spent many balmy evenings together! A young lady selling dairy products ensured that we always had something to eat. The lady from the music distributors ensured that we always had the latest and the best music at our regular late night get togethers while the lingerie doll made sure that we were never short of gentlemen's entertainment.

Part of our work entailed calling on hospitals where the neatly uniformed nurses were a major attraction too. Night shifts were a good time to visit the hospitals. Most of the hospitals were pretty quiet after 10pm and we were able to meet in the kitchen where we could have tea and a midnight snack at the government's expense while enjoying some really pleasant company. Although we were proud of our status as medical reps we were in fact just traveling salesmen. So I understood what the cat meant. The cat? Yes. When the kittens asked their mother who their father was she replied: "Your daddy was a travelling man."

There was seldom a dull moment. On one occasion I returned to my car to find someone scratching in the boot. What really irked me was that this apparent thief was going about it in a leisurely manner.

Theft and hijacking were already the order of the day. Wasting no time I rushed up and clobbered him with my bag full of medical samples. It was quite a heavy bag. Although I aimed at his head, I only managed to bring it down on his left shoulder. He swung around and pointed his finger at me as one would do with a gun. It was at this moment that a terrible truth struck me. This was not my car! Yes it was blue and yes, it was a Ford Cortina. Oh dear! My car, I then saw, was parked just two bays further up the line! I stood back, put my hands in the air and apologized profusely. Fortunately the "offender" turned out to be a gentleman. He accepted my apologies. All this took place much to the amusement of the onlookers who should have been charged for the matinee performance!

On another occasion in yet another case of mistaken identity, I struggled for five minutes not knowing why my car key would not unlock the door. Finally it dawned on me that I had it in the keyhole of someone else's car! Luckily the owner did not pitch up while I was unwittingly attempting to get into his car. On this occasion my car was parked right next to the one I was trying to open.

After two years of traveling and at the age of twenty-eight, I suddenly decided to stop philandering. It was time to take a wife and settle down. Good idea. Bad mistake. I married a young lass six years my junior. Although the decision to marry was an intellectual one I was dating three girls at the time and who will ever know if I made the right choice. From an intellectual point of view I think I did. Romantically I do not believe that people fall in love. They fall in lust. Hence the terminology, "she fell pregnant." Anyhow, after a whirlwind romance a wedding date was set and my life was due to undergo a major change. This change was so dramatic that for two decades I forgot about the box. Perhaps it was my mother-in-law who saw me in the box and got the idea to bind it firmly with glad wrap so that I would be so stifled that I did not even have a desire to escape.

Married life was good. After two years we had a son. Two years later we had a daughter. A year later tragedy struck. Our son died in a drowning accident. We were devastated. I will never forget the day of his funeral. It was a pristine autumn day. The sky was azure. I can't recall ever seeing such a perfectly beautiful blue sky before. There wasn't a cloud in the sky. There wasn't even a breeze. The heat of the summer had passed and the cold of the winter had not yet come. The day seemed as perfect as the innocence of the little three-year-old body that lay in his little white coffin. Two days after the funeral our family left us and we were on our own. It was scary and we were terribly lonely. We had only been living in our new house for six months and it was sparsely furnished. Suddenly it seemed very bare and our lives seemed very, very empty. Having not been in the area long, we had not yet made friends. We did not even know our neighbours. We had no telephone. The night after our respective families left the first signs of winter set in. That night it started to rain and the tears ran uncontrollably down my cheeks in sympathy with the rain. Or was it God shedding some tears in sympathy with us? The very thought of Quinton lying out there alone in the cold and wet cemetery burnt a hole in my heart. A part of me died and remained dead for two and a half years.

Life goes on. Slowly we pulled ourselves out of the depth of despair. Slowly we started to live again. It wasn't easy. Exactly two and a half years after our little boy's death we were blessed with a second daughter. This truly was the start of a new chapter in our lives. Two little girls. Two bundles of joy. Yes, I wanted to call her Joy because I could see that the joy she brought into her mother's life was just that – sheer joy. It was equaled only by my own joy. My grandmother's name had been Joy. I didn't like my grandmother very much. So we called our little bundle of joy Juanita. At least we got the J right. We decided to pronounce her name the Spanish way. Phonetically that is Wanita. At least that is one thing about the English language. You can't put it in a box. Spelling and pronunciation don't always go hand in hand. Juanita proved to be a truly delightful child. Always obedient. Always willing to go the extra mile. Two years later my wife had a little boy. Our lives seemed to be on track.

The pharmaceutical industry was good to me. I had been promoted into a middle management position. I now had what was mainly an office job. There was still traveling to be done. Now it was mainly a matter of flying around the country at regular intervals. Then there was the annual overseas trip for further training. This was good. Once more I was on top of the world.

Funny though. Everything in life seems to work in cycles. Without intending to do so I must have tramped on some toes. It was at this time of our lives that my wife and I changed faith for the fifth time in our married life. We became reborn Christians. You see, subliminally, I guess my search for the opening in the box was still going on. We found a great deal of peace with the "happy-clappy's." These were the Charismatic Baptists that we had joined.

Some of the senior management at the company I was working for did not approve of my new found religious affiliation. Inevitably when well-meaning colleagues warned me of sharpening knives I did not believe them. More is the pity. Things started going wrong. I do not know what it is about religion but it seems to bring out both the best and the worst in people. My open criticism of a romantic affair between the married marketing manager and one of my juniors did not go down well. Neither of them had any religious convictions while I was going through a "holier than thou" phase. I thought that I could say what I liked so long as it was true. God was my witness. He was on my side. He would protect me. He did not. Matters took a serious turn for the worse when the young lady was promoted in a leap frog movement. From being my junior she was now my senior. Suddenly she was my line manager, my boss. As we had never seen eye to eye I may as well have resigned on the spot. What had been a good career with one of the leading international pharmaceutical houses was about to turn sour. Very sour.

Miss Crash set about making my life hell. Six months later I walked out.

No problem though. I had been in the industry for almost 20 years. I had a good name. Soon I had another management position with another international pharmaceutical company. The pay was even better. My mother was right: "When one door closes another door opens." But I was still stuck in the damn box!

It was during the next five years that the scales of innocence fell from my eyes regarding the pharmaceutical industry. As I grew in my new position I was exposed to people and to closely guarded secrets that I had not even considered previously. I learnt that the industry had its own mafia. Their members infiltrated every level of the industry. They had people on their payroll and at all levels. They had "friends" in politics. They had "friends" in the Ministry of Health. They controlled tenders and the prices of medicine. They penetrated every single pharmaceutical wholesaler and all the large private pharmaceutical manufacturers and importers. They had members at every level within the major companies from top management down to the sales force and truck drivers. "What did they do? How did they do it" Let us start with the question, "what did they do?" They made themselves very rich. How did they do it? The first inkling I got of this was from Mr. Badrum. This man appeared as the ultimate gentleman. Always prim. Always proper. Hand made Italian shoes made of the softest leather. Suits to match. At that stage in time the pharmaceutical companies had what is known as different exit prices. This meant that a product would be sold to the wholesaler at one price, to retail chemists at another price, to dispensing doctors at a different price and to the government institutions at yet another price. Now this is where the whole system opened its doors to abuse. Imagine this: the agreed price of a product called "Cough-a-lot" is sold to the wholesalers for twenty dollars. The same product is sold to the government hospitals for two dollars. Mr. Badrum organizes for an order of 100 000 bottles to be dispatched to the local hospital at two dollars per bottle. Somehow this order ends up on the shelves of the local wholesaler who should have paid twenty dollars a bottle. I never quite figured out the intricacies of how this was done. What I do know is that it was done. How do I know this? I was responsible for sales to the wholesaler. On one of my regular visits to the same I suddenly saw far more "Cough-a-lot" on his shelves than he ordered from me in a year and I knew he was selling it. Statistics proved that. So how did the mafia benefit from this? I guess each member got a share but it doesn't take a rocket scientist to figure out that 20-2 x 100 000 equals a lot of dollars. And this was only one of a range of hundreds of products. I started to understand why Mr. Badrum's children went to the best private schools, why he had two holiday homes, why he kept only Johnny Walker Blue Label and Chivas Regal Twelve year old in his private bar.

I knew that neither his nor his wife's parents were well off. I knew what his salary was. As I have said before I am good with arithmetic. Two plus two does not equal ten. Sadly for his family, Mr. Badrum was killed in a hijacking some years later. Or was it a hijacking? Perhaps someone got greedy. Perhaps someone did not get his share. Either way, it is irrelevant. There is always someone around ready to step into a dead man's shoes. As the local saying goes – one man's death is another man's meal ticket!

During my five years with this company I traveled extensively. I learned the "importance" of buying the support of the top specialists in various fields. To get a so-called opinion maker on one's side it was sometimes necessary to entertain them lavishly. On one occasion I was ordered to take a particular specialist to Singapore to attend a one-week medical congress. The company paid for both our airfares as well as Dr. Moon's wife, all first class and five star accommodation. The company also covered meals and entertainment for the three of us. What did Dr. Moon have to do? He had to give a thirty-minute talk on the Thursday morning using the name of one of our company's products in a positive way. He had to use it at least five times. What did I have to do? I had to see that Dr. Moon's every wish was pandered to and that his wife was well looked after while he was talking. He had a beautiful wife and I wished his talk had to carry on the whole day and through the night! It did not. The day after I returned from this, my second Singapore trip, tragedy struck our family again.

Our seventeen-year-old daughter was killed in a car accident. We were totally devastated. How my dear wife got through the years that followed I will never know. As for me? I went to pieces. I could not concentrate on my work. I lost touch with my two remaining children. How did they cope? I don't know. My little girl was dead. The bottom fell out of my box. Had I been trying too hard to get out of the top? My life was empty. I was no longer interested in the box. Was God telling me to conform? I read a book called "Why bad things happen to good people." It did not help. I shouted at my two remaining children for watching television programs that I did not like. That did not help either. I felt guilty about my daughter's death. Very guilty. Who was that idiot in the bible who failed to discipline his children? Eli. Had I been too lenient with my daughter? Had I failed as a parent – again? The fellow in the bible fell over backwards and broke his neck. Would God punish me likewise? I wished he would. He did not. Everyday I woke up with a feeling of emptiness. I could not look my wife in the eye. She was grieving her way. I was not grieving. I was bitter.

There was another reason for my guilt feelings. Our daughter was not killed outright in that automobile accident. When we were called to the hospital she was still alive. We were excited. We were going to see her. She was going to be okay. Maybe she had some broken bones, some scratches, some bruises? They would heal. Before we were permitted to see her we were told that the neurologist wished to see us. My blood went cold. I shivered. What was wrong? The neurologist quietly explained that we could see her in a few minutes. Then followed the punch that knocked us out. "Your daughter is brain dead. Her body is fine. She has no broken bones. No cuts. No bruises. She looks fine. She is on life support. She took a severe blow to her head. After you have seen her please come back to me. You may go and see her now."

Trembling we moved to the ward where our daughter lay. She looked like sleeping beauty. We could not believe that the next time we would see her would be in a coffin. When we returned to the neurologist he said that there was no chance of her recovering. He asked us to sign release papers donating her healthy organs for transplants to people in need of them. As we had discussed the matter of organ transplants with our children a week prior to our daughter's accident we knew she would approve. We signed and it was all over. Then doubt set in. Had we made the right decision? Had I made the right decision? It was very magnanimous of us to consider the welfare of others but what of our daughter? What if the neurologist was wrong? I felt like I thought Pontius Pilate must have felt after he condemned Jesus to death. Had I just condemned my own daughter to death? The agony was unbearable. The pain incurable.

Unlike Pontius Pilate, I could not wash my hands. Then I remembered the story of the man who had been bitten by a Mamba. It made me feel worse. The mamba is an extremely venomous snake found in Africa. Its venom deadens the nerves. It causes paralysis of the respiratory tract which usually leads to a very rapid death. If the victim is kept quiet and he can be put on a respirator very soon after the bite he may survive. After a mamba had bitten the man, he was on the point of death when his friend got him to a top class hospital. The doctors connected him to a ventilator. He had already lost consciousness. The respirator kept him breathing. He remained unconscious for weeks. When his system finally got rid of the venom and his natural breathing finally took over again he told a scary story.

Most of the time that he was in a coma, he was aware of what was happening around him. He could hear and understand what doctors and visitors said. He just could not breathe on his own and he could not move a muscle. He says he could hear the doctors discussing his condition and telling his family that he would probably not recover.

They discussed switching off the respirator. That really scared him. He recovered the day before they were due to flick the switches. Was our daughter aware of her condition? Could she see us? Was she crying out for help but unable to make herself heard? The very thought was too much to bear. But the deed was done. Two days after the hospital authorities got our signature the transplants were done. We found out later that in such cases the organs are removed while the donor is still alive. This makes medical sense because the recipient is then assured of the freshest possible organs. Both donor and recipient are wheeled into the operating theatre. The recipient's malfunctioning organ is then removed and the new one taken from the donor and transplanted immediately.

Eventually we were told to go to the state mortuary to identify our daughter's body. I did not see my way clear to do this. I had identified our three-year-old son's little body sixteen years earlier. To be called upon to identify the body of one's child is the most painful thing any parent can be asked to do. To be asked to do it twice was more than I could bear. A family friend who was a pastor at the time agreed to stand in for me. He also performed the funeral service.

I spiraled into a state of severe depression. My work suffered. I could not cope. In spite of putting on a brave front and going on two more overseas trips for the company – one to Brazil and one to Austria – I was losing my grip. Besides these trips there was also a lot of local traveling to do. This meant up to a week at a time away from home.

The plane trips. The five star hotels. The dazzling evenings out. The entertainment. All this lost its glitter. All I wanted to do was to be at home with my wife and two younger children. The company insisted that I pull myself together. The Marketing Manager (my immediate superior), a man whose closest brush with death was the peaceful passing of his grandmother, was particularly unsympathetic. He did not even pretend to understand my pain. He merely pointed out how the financial manager had "overcome" the death of his son. This boy had committed suicide at the age of twenty. The father had taken two weeks compassionate leave and returned to his cloistered office. He had no need to travel or address large meetings or deal with difficult customers. Each person's pain is different. I did not wish to draw comparisons. My superior did. I got fed up. I refused to go on the next two overseas trips that were pushed my way. That did it! I was asked to leave. I did not contest this. I was glad to write out my letter of resignation.

Thus ended my twenty five years in the Pharmaceutical Industry.

Chapter Eleven

Unemployed

What followed immediately after my departure from the Pharmaceutical Industry was eighteen months of desolation. I cut myself off from the outside world. I drew into my shell. After a year I was more tightly boxed in than ever before. Not only was I boxed but I was also bottled. I totally forgot that I once abhorred the very idea of alcohol abuse. I forgot the beautiful example my teetotalling parents had set for me. I forgot how I had despised the university lecturer who had been a heavy drinker and had punished me for winning Berthildt's favours. I was caught in a trough of depression. I drank too much. Far too much. I did too little. Far too little. For the first year I had no income. We were living off my savings. When this ran out I sold my trailer. Then I sold my car. Then I sold my wife's much loved childhood piano. Then I took a mortgage on our home. Then I was penniless. At the age of fifty-two I was flat out broke. At the age of fifty-three I had lost what I had worked for my whole life long. Then I remembered the church where we had worshipped and tithed and given our free gift offerings for so many years. I swallowed my pride and approached the church for help. This proved a worthless exercise.

Three month's later I was still jobless and still penniless. By this time I had pulled myself together sufficiently to start looking for work again. As job application after job application was turned down, I started to lose faith in humanity. After day in and day out of walking the streets, knocking on doors and asking every doctor, receptionist and pharmacist I had ever gotten to know during my time in the pharmaceutical industry hope failed me. I started to lose faith in myself.

Depression set in once more. I had a few good insurance policies. I did my sums. If I died my wife and children would be well provided for. They would not go hungry. The children would finish their education. The house would be paid for! Having now lost all faith in humanity, the church and myself, what was I to do? Where was I to turn? I had even lost faith in God's representatives – the priests, the pastors, the ministers of religion.

Desperate times calls for desperate measures. I decided to approach God directly. Furthermore, I decided to call the odds. It may sound threatening to you. It may even sound disrespectful but I took a chance. I said to God:

"I need a job. I need an income. Your representatives have let me down. My church brothers have forsaken me. My friends have turned their backs on me. My life is now in your hands. If you cannot, if you do not organize a job for me I will kill myself."

I did not leave it at that. I carried on by saying to God: "If you have not done this for me by the 29th of December (my late daughter's birthday) I will kill myself."

Not giving God much time, I left it at that. My short but powerful emotionally laid one-way communication with God was over.

I mentioned to my wife what I had done - my bargain with God himself. I also told her that it was now up to him. I stopped applying for work and put my brain into neutral and my life on hold. I waited.

Two weeks before the 29th my wife came home one night after attending a prayer meeting with a circle of her friends. She had told them of our plight. One friend of hers said:

"My boss, a factory owner, is looking for a sales manager. Go home and get your husband's curriculum vitae. I will give it to my boss tomorrow, who knows?"

The next day Mr. Plesser phoned me. He said he had read my curriculum vitae and would like to talk to me. At the interview he made it clear that the job was not a popular one and that the pay was poor. He asked me what the very minimum was that I was prepared to settle for. At that stage I was truly desperate. I was prepared to settle for next to nothing. I also knew that one was more likely to get a job when you had a job. So at the very least I saw this as a stepping stone back into the job market.

It is a funny thing about prospective employers but they generally prefer an applicant who is presently employed. We struck a deal. I had a job.

During the short time I had left before starting this job, my mind turned to some of the things that had taken place while I was unemployed. The one thing that struck home more deeply than any other was the rejection that I had suffered at the hand of the church. It really riled me to think of all the hours that I had spent attending church services and the thousands of dollars I had given to the church over the years. Yet when I was in need I got no material help whatsoever.

Chapter Twelve

Fortunes out of Christianity

I had first hand experience with the Charismatic Baptists in the art of giving and receiving. Their philosophy is simple. You give. They receive. End of story. Yet I guess they could learn a lot from the Pope and his gang about hoarding.

The prime example of people making fortunes out of religion must be the Roman Catholic Church with its undisclosed riches estimated by various authorities to be in the region of not billions but trillions of dollars. All those riches are hoarded by the keepers of gold and jewels in the Vatican City while the happy givers, the millions of devout and not so devout Catholics, go forth and live in poverty and produce many more children than they can afford, because the church still frowns on the pill as a means of birth control.

The Charismatic Baptists of today are also real money-making machines. They rake in more money on a Sunday than most casinos do in a week. Give, give, give and you will be blessed. That is their motto. What shall I give you may ask?

They are clear on that. You must give one tenth of your earnings. That is your obligation as decreed by God. Then there are the free gifts and offerings that you need to give. This is what really determines the position you will attain in heaven one day; the tithe is merely your entry ticket!

What does God do with all this money? Remember the pastors tell you it is for God's work. You are not giving to the pastors. Oh, no. You are giving to God. So what does He do? They tell you he looks after the poor. He will ensure that the meek shall inherit the earth. How does he look after the poor? He feeds and clothes them. How does he do this? Through his servants, the pastors of his sheep. Who are the sheep? You and I are the sheep. We who give our wool in spite of the cold.

The leaders of the more conservative churches are no less guilty. When I was newly married my mother-in-law prevailed upon me to join her faith. She was a member of the Dutch Reformed Church. Here I became a member of the church board. It was at their meetings that I was first exposed to some of the corruption that goes on behind closed church doors. Being a conservative church probably explains why their corruption and misuse of church funds was of a more conservative nature. Everything had to be above board and accounted for. What bothered me though were questions like:- "Why did the dominee (minister) have to earn a salary twice that of the bank manager? Why did he live in a rent free house paid for out of church funds tithed by the members? Why did the church pay his lights and water account? How come he drove the latest model Mercedes Benz when most of the congregation went to work by bus or bicycle? Why did the ladies group at the church always have to cater for his wife's functions and why were they not compensated for their time, effort and money spent?" Oh, I forgot. They will be rewarded in heaven one day! Pie in the sky!

Now I know that religious people like testimonies. They like us to tell our stories. They like to hear how we were healed. They like to share these testimonies of healing with new converts. So here is my testimony: -

I was a devout member of such a church for five years. I gave liberally. I tithed every month. There were 6000 members in our congregation. I am good at arithmetic and I worked out the following sum one day. If every member tithed and they earned only half of what I earned, wow! The church (the pastor/God) was receiving 3000 tenths or 300 times a month what I was receiving. (Remember that a tithe is one tenth of one's gross income) That was a great deal of money. It could help many people.

In the days of Moses the people were divided into groups of ten and each group of ten had a religious leader, advisor, pastor. Now that makes mathematical sense because if each one of those ten gave a tenth of their income to the pastor he would have an income equal to the average of their individual incomes. Presumably he gave a tenth of his income to his superior and so forth. That is pretty fair. Yes, equal seems fair. What do you think when the guy you are giving one tenth of your income to is collecting 300 times your gross salary every month?

Well, let me continue with my testimony. I had a jolly good job and I was earning a very good salary. Then I fell upon bad times. I lost my job. I had to sell my house and car. My pride would not let me beg. After six months I was almost destitute. As a last resort I turned to God. I could not find Him. So I went to the pastor. Remember, I had been tithing at his church for five years. That equals sixty months. Forget about all the free gifts and offerings I had made in that time. Just take one tenth of sixty months and that equals six months full salary. That is before tax and other deductions. Well, I thought, the pastor would help me. I told him my plight. "Oh, yes," he said "Do not despair, God has the answer. Praise the Lord. Hallelujah! Amen! Come brother, let us pray." Ten minutes later, hungry and thirsty, I went on my weary way. I saw the pastor locking up his Mercedes in his garage as I left. I saw him go into his home. I saw him pour himself a drink. Then he drew the curtains and I saw him no more. I walked the fifteen miles home in the dark.

Do you find it strange that I've never been back? It was that night that the truth came to me. Walking home in the dark I realized who the pastor really was. He was not God's messenger. He was not doing God's work. He was a wolf in sheep's clothing! He was a devil in disguise. Believe me, friend, he has many brothers out there. They are all gathering tithes and free gift offerings. They are doing it in the name of the Lord. Go and look at the houses they live in. Go and look at the cars they drive. Go and see if they are living with their first or second wife. Go and see which brothels they are visiting.

Chapter Thirteen

Selling Coffins

To pick up from where I left off before being carried away and going on about crooked priests. By the way, I have subsequently found that there are some honest people wearing the cloth. In fact a large number of priests and pastors are genuinely interested in doing good. I guess it's the proverbial bad apple that had me thinking that the whole barrel was rotten. It's not!

Anyhow, a short recap. After being jobless for over a year I said to God: "I've had enough. On the 29th of December (that was my late daughter's birthday) I am going to kill myself unless you get me a job. I need a job. I need to earn money. I've still got a wife and I've got two children at school. PLEASE HELP ME."

So do you know what He did? Now I want you to know before I tell you how God helped me, that I am an educated man with various university degrees and diplomas and with considerable management expertise and international experience. Most of this in the fields of education and medicine. But do you know what God does? He gets me a job as a coffin salesman – selling coffins! Can you think of anything more morbid? But God in strange ways His miracles performs.

My first day at my new job turned out to be most enlightening in a very depressing way (excuse the mixed metaphor). I reported to Mr. Plesser at five minutes to eight o'clock sharp. I really pride myself on my good time keeping. My father used to say: "Son, never be late for an appointment. Be early. Never be late. If you are less than five minutes early consider that as being late."

This advice had stood me in good stead in both my business and private life. Thus I felt good, as I was about to make a favourable impression on the factory owner. He looked at me with a grin rather than a smile and said, "You are late. We start at seven o'clock here!"

Oh dear, oh dear! What was meant to be a good start turned out to be a bad start! I also discovered that although my job title was that of "Sales Manager", and although I was to be in charge of three junior salesmen, my job would in fact be that of a senior salesman looking after the company's most important customers. So Mr. Plesser had driven a hard bargain. He was getting both a sales manager and a salesman for the price of just one employee. Beggars can't be choosers. I decided to keep my silence and do my best. I soon learned that Mr Plesser was generally known to the staff as Mr Scrooge and I also learned why.

As the front office door was only opened at 07h30 by the receptionist, the staff had to enter via the factory and warehouse. This meant parking in a really dirty backyard full of wood off-cuts and shavings as well as scrap metal left behind by the previous tenants. Walking through the factory was depressing. Everywhere there were coffins at various stages of manufacture. Having passed through the factory it was then necessary to negotiate a long passage before arriving at the stairwell to my office. On either side of this passage there were rows and rows of coffins piled up to the ceiling which was very high indeed, about three to four storeys! Lighting in both the factory and the warehouse was dim. Mr. Plesser did not believe in wasting! On the way up to my office there was yet another morbid sight. The mezzanine was used by an old lady who did the lining and padding of the coffins. This old bird, no taller than five foot two, looked like death warmed up. She reminded me of the witch in "Hansel and Gretel." She had an interesting spark in her one eye though and her crooked little forefinger on the right hand seemed to beckon one. It seemed to say, "Come here. Come and look. I have got a nice coffin for you. See how soft the lining is. It is padded. It is cozy. Come and lie in this coffin my dear. It is for you!"

After the first day I made a point of being at the factory door at a quarter to seven every morning. In winter it was still dark and walking through the silent factory and warehouse did in no way compare to the flashing lights of Broadway!

Factory work is dirty work. Working with wood, and especially with the cheaper chip wood from which most coffins are made, is a very dirty affair. There are wood shavings and there is sawdust everywhere. It gets into everything. For this reason the workers were provided with showers so that they could clean themselves up at the end of a hard day's work.

Health and safety regulations demanded this. When I said to Mr. Plesser that there was no hot water he said: "Yes, I know. I keep the geyser turned off. It uses electricity. The law requires that I provide the workers with washing facilities and with water. It does not say anything about hot water."

I thought this to be inhumane, but like the factory workers, I was not in a position to bargain. Showering in cold water in winter as the sun was setting made most of the men look like little boys. Well, parts of them, anyhow. I did not see for myself but I was told that the icy water in winter even brought new exciting dimensions to the women's breasts! We had to find something to smile about.

The factory operated from seven in the morning until five in the afternoon, a half hour break for lunch and two fifteen minute tea breaks. I worked out that that still meant a nine-hour working day which was one hour longer than the eight hours permitted by law. Mr. Plesser did not pay overtime. Most of his factory labourers were either aliens or illegal immigrants so they did not complain. One of the drivers who was hired to deliver coffins could neither read nor speak the local language. When I asked one of his colleagues how he managed I was told that on his first trip he was taken out by a driver who knew the route. After that he just had to remember.

After a brief introduction to the coffin business, I hit the road. Mr. Plesser said that I should not think of coffins as a place for dead people.

"No," he said "just see them as boxes." So I set off to see my first customers. No, we did not supply the end users! I guess this is one business where you really do need a middle man. The middle man in this business is the undertaker.

So off I went to see my first undertaker. Was I nervous? Yes. Did I enjoy the experience? No! There is something about the inside of an undertaker's business that is different to any other. There is a solemnity about the place. It does not seem alive. It seems empty. Most undertakers have premises consisting of three parts while some have four or even five. In America they are called funeral homes. The typical undertaker has a reception area where you are made to feel as comfortable as I suppose one can under such circumstances. This consists of a reception desk with a receptionist who is often of the older variety. It seems most younger girls are not attracted to dealing with death.

The reception area is usually furnished with a few comfortable lounge chairs and is decorated with beautiful wreaths and comforting sympathy cards. From the reception area one passes to the display room. This is where you can look at a range of the most up to date and most expensive coffins and caskets. They are all immaculately lined and come with a choice of shrouds. Only if you cannot afford one of the coffins on display will the undertaker condescend to taking you into his warehouse. Here you will find the less expensive coffins, even simple pine boxes with rope handles especially made for the Jewish fraternity. The cheapest of all and what he will not show you unless you ask, is a coffin liner. This is usually made of the very cheapest chipboard and is essentially designed to fit into a casket. Why? If you are to be cremated you can hire an expensive casket. The body of the deceased is placed inside the liner, which is placed inside the casket. The very expensive casket your wife has organized for you will impress your family and friends. No one needs to know that it will be going back to the show room after the church service. No one needs to know that you will burn to ashes in a simple chipboard liner. In some areas chipboard may not be used in the crematorium because of the air pollution caused by the glue used in the manufacture of the chipboard. In these instances the cheapest thinnest local pine or saligna is used. Saligna is a type of eucalyptus. It is seldom used for the manufacture of coffins because it has a tendency to warp. It burns well though!

Most reputable undertakers have a mortuary on site. This is usually hidden at the back of the building. Why? Well, this is where the body of the deceased is kept refrigerated. It is also where the undertaker does the final preparation of the body before the family come for a viewing. Another less obvious reason why it is hidden from the public view is because it is often right next to your favourite restaurant facing the other street. If not a restaurant then perhaps the baker or the butcher? Sobering thought! Perhaps a bottle store would be more hygienic? There is not much difference between alcohol and embalming fluid!

Finally there may be a small chapel. This is for use should the deceased or his family have no religious affiliation and no loving caring pastor to do the honours. Here anyone can perform a service. It is amazing that one needs to be registered with the council of churches to perform a wedding service. It is also interesting that one needs to write an examination to get a government license in order to marry people. Yet anyone can perform a funeral service and anyone can bury you!

The geographical area I was to cover was huge. It stretched from Gaberone in Botswana on the western front to Manzini in Swaziland in the east. Northwards we serviced clients as far afield as Musina in the Limpopo Province and in the south we went as far as Bloemfontein and Roosendal. Some of these trips meant covering a distance of over 800 kilometres in one day. Visits to Mbabane and Manzini were particularly taxing. They meant leaving home at 04h30 in order to be at the border post when it opened at eight. On one occasion I had a few coffins on the back of my pick-up truck for delivery to a customer in Manzini. I was already halfway to the border when I remembered that I had forgotten the documents necessary for "import/export" at home. As I was crossing an international border these papers were essential. I was in no mood to turn back and so decided to push my luck. The border patrol officers on the South African side let me through after some sweet talk. On the Swaziland side it was not so easy and I was ordered to park my vehicle and wait. After being interrogated as to where I was going and why and how long I would be, I was told to wait some more.

After about an hour one of the senior officers approached me and said:"I too am going to Manzini. I am off duty now. I need a lift. Let's go!" Now was that not nice?

Selling coffins proved highly profitable. Within three months I was earning more than I had been earning as National Sales Manager of forty-nine people. Now I had only three junior sales people to worry about. Sure I spent most of my time travelling. This was a totally different field though. It was far less stressful. After six months Mr. Scrooge (that is Mr. Plesser) rewarded my efforts. When I first started he based my income on a percentage of coffins sold and paid for. In a way this also made me a debt collector! Initially my commission was 1.83% of coffins sold and paid for. After six months this was increased to 1.94%. Soon my wife and I were enjoying a fairly comfortable life style again. There was something to smile about. By and large though it was hard work.

On one occasion I left the factory with a full load of coffins. These were for two customers. The first was some 200 kilometres and the second a further 150 kilometres from base. The factory workers knew how to stack the maximum number of coffins onto any vehicle and secure them firmly. The lower twelve were for the more distant undertaker while the top eight were for my first stop. The lower twelve were top of the range solid kiaat, imbuia and mahogany. These were fully trimmed with handles. They were really heavy. The upper eight were lightweight chipboard and untrimmed. Some undertakers preferred to do their own trimming to save on cost. These coffins therefore had no handles or lining.

After arriving at my first stop, I went in to talk to the undertaker and do the necessary paperwork. I also had to do a stock take as we sold our coffins on a consignment basis. Any coffins used by the undertaker since my previous visit now had to be paid for. While busy with this the undertaker's staff off-loaded his new stock and secured the balance of the coffins on my vehicle. Business done I set off on the next leg of my journey. Some thirty kilometres on, a friendly passer by waved at me. I waved back. The next three cars to pass me all waved wildly and I thought: "What lovely friendly people there are in this neighbourhood!"

My truck seemed to be leaning to the left and I put that down to the camber of the road. Then a group of schoolchildren that I passed not only waved but also pointed to the coffins and dispersed into the maize field on the side of the road. I thought again to myself: "See, children really are scared of death. They must think I am transporting a load of bodies!" My truck was now seriously pulling to the left. I decided to stop. Just in time too. Those idiots at my first stop had not secured my load properly and I had failed to check. So who was the real idiot? The top layer of my load had moved way over to the left. These were very heavy coffins and my efforts to move them back into place was fruitless. I needed help. The first and only car to respond to my frantic waving had two young men in it. Was I glad to see them! It was winter. There was an icy wind and the sun was starting to set. When the two young men got out of the car and realized what my load was they turned pale, jumped back into their car and sped off! I started to panic. I did not fancy spending a cold winter's night on the side of the road. Cell phones were only just being introduced and I did not have one. At that stage they were very expensive and considered a luxury. What was I to do? Then an angel appeared in the form of a labourer on a bicycle. I begged and pleaded with him to help me. It did not work. He said he too needed to move on before it got dark. I offered him money. He still said: "No!" I doubled and then trebled my offer. He finally answered: "Yes!"

Forty-five minutes later and with my supper money gone I set off with my load back in place and reasonably well secured. From this point on I travelled very slowly and kept a close watch in my rear view mirrors. Soon it was pitch dark and freezing. I arrived at my small town destination at 9:30pm.

Everything in town was closed. I pulled up outside the undertaker's front door. I was dirty and tired and cold. Fortunately I had a blanket, which I used to cover the plastic seat of the truck. Fortunately the truck was so old that it still had a bench seat. This allowed me to curl up on the seat as best I could, cover myself with the blanket and sleep. It was a fitful sleep and a cold uncomfortable one. At 8 o'clock sharp the next morning the undertaker arrived. He was very understanding and gave me a cup of hot coffee before taking me to his nearby house to freshen up in his bathroom before returning to his parlour to complete our business. Two hours later I was on my way home. As cold as I was that night I recall another occasion when the heat really got to me.

A trip to Botswana in mid summer is a very hot and very dry experience. My vehicle did not have air conditioning. Mr. Scrooge saw no need for that. There also was no radio in the vehicle. I still had no mobile phone. I was to meet a new customer at a crossing just outside Gaberone, the capital city of Botswana. We had agreed to meet at noon. Mrs Fairbottom, the undertaker, had invited me for lunch at her house. After waiting at the cross roads for almost an hour in the heat of a very dry and dusty day I drove into the city in search of a pay phone. She answered on the first ring and told me that her husband had been waiting for me for an hour just 500 yards from where I had been sitting in the midday sun. And you thought only mad dogs and Englishmen go out in the midday sun! An hour later, hot and embarrassed I was sitting on their front porch. With a gin and tonic in one hand we settled down to a meal of cold meat and salad. Since it was now past 1.30pm and extremely hot and dry and since the food had been prepared for serving at noon the meat was no longer cold and moist but it was warm, dry and curling up at the edges. Myriads of dark green bottle flies seemed to enjoy it though.

The "fresh" salad was now limp and unattractive. The gin and tonic was good though. We ate little and drank much. Their house was on the very outskirts of the city and monkeys gambolled in the shade of a nearby tree. We finished our drinks and finished our business. I had to leave in time to get back across the border before it closed at 6pm. Then there was still a 400 km journey home. Mr Plesser did not approve of sleeping at hotels or guest houses. The rule was that if you did not have friends or family en route you ought to get back to your own bed. The seat belt on my vehicle chaffed against my skin. It was so hot I had loosened my shirt. I arrived home at 10pm. When I awoke the next morning I was covered in blisters caused by the heat and the chafing of the seat belt against my skin.

Those long trips also had their benefits. They gave me time to think. Slowly I started to get my life together again. Having no radio to listen to while driving I was able to turn my thoughts to God. The roads were mostly quiet and driving was a pleasure. My bakkie was so old that I could not exceed the national speed limit of 120kmh even if I tried. For long stretches between towns and villages I could therefore give my full attention to life. Slowly I started to wiggle my way out of the box. I was now a true loner. At least for a few hours at a time and for three or four days every week. What did that mean? I no longer belonged to a minority group. Being alone meant that I had a majority of one! That put me in charge! That was good to know. I no longer needed to conform. My thoughts were set free. Questions that came to mind were: "Did Jesus die on the cross?" and "Do dead men bleed?"

The latter question was the easier to answer. Working with people who work with the dead gave me an interest in the question. It also raised many other questions about death.

After two and a half years of selling coffins I had come to realize just how many people are affected by death and in particular by the death of a child. It is not natural for children to die before their parents and that is why it is so very hard to accept. Dealing with undertakers on a daily basis made me realize that many, many, many parents had given up one or more children to the angel of death. My wife and I were not alone in our suffering. While this stark fact did not alleviate our pain it did do something to help just knowing that we were not alone. It is often said that a burden shared is a burden halved. The fact that we were not alone somehow eased the pain a little.

It was at this point that something profound happened in my life. It proved to be a life changing experience. This is what transpired:-

It was ten o'clock on a crispy winter's morning. It was a typical winter windless day with clear blue skies. It reminded me of the day we buried our son. I called on an undertaker in the usual way but what was about to take place was not usual. He was very busy and a little irritable. He said to me: "I can't stop to talk today. I have a funeral at 2:30 this afternoon. I still have to prepare the body. The family is coming at twelve. If you want to talk to me you will have to come to the back room with me and talk while I work."

Without further ado he went through the parlour to the back room. I followed like a little puppy dog. As he bent over to start his work on the young face he said: "This girl was killed in a car accident. She was only seventeen. I had to fetch her body from Pretoria. Just got back!" I moved closer and saw the girl's face. My daughter had been killed in a car accident. It had also happened in Pretoria some 60 kilometers away. My daughter had also been seventeen. This child also had long blond hair and a pale complexion with a blemish free skin. I went cold. I was looking at my daughter. I was doing what I should have done almost six years previously. I was identifying her body. When I left that parlour that morning a great peace came over me. I had found closure. God had worked his miracle.

Now I do not believe that anyone who has lost a child ever experiences complete closure. Nevertheless, I had found a serene peace that I had not known since my daughter's death.

God had worked his miracle in my life. Following this experience I lost interest in my work. It had served its purpose. I was able to worm my way out of the box. I resigned a month later to start my own business.

Besides the great miracle that God brought my way through the funeral business I also learned that dead men don't bleed.

Chapter Fourteen

Dead men don't bleed

How do you know when you are dead? Well, that is no problem. You know it. You are no longer bound by the confines of your physical body. You are free. You are free to go where the spirit leads you. If you are an advanced soul you are at peace and go almost anywhere you please. If you are a young soul you still have much to learn and may still feel tethered but you will be guided once you realize where you are and what has happened to your body - that is, that you have left it, and are no longer bound by its restrictions.

The real question is – how do other people know that you are dead? Your loved ones do not want you to be dead. Most people still flounder under the illusion that it is better to be alive. For that reason they will not accept your death until a medical doctor pronounces you dead. How does he know that you are dead? Firstly you will have stopped breathing. The doctor will place his hand or a mirror or glass at your nostrils to observe any expulsion of air. Secondly your pulse will stop. Your heart will stop pumping. These are two very important measurements of death but they are not fool proof. It is possible for the human to go some minutes without breathing and still live. After the brain has been without oxygen for a certain time due to the lack of breath the brain starts to die. When the heart stops pumping you are also at death's door. This does not mean that you are dead. Modern medicine has revived millions of people whose hearts have stopped beating either due to a heart attack or heart failure during or after an operation.

In days gone by you were buried with a bell in your coffin just in case you were not really dead. This allowed you to ring the bell in case of you waking up in the dark and hopefully someone would hear the bell and come to your rescue.

There are many tales of people who were pronounced dead or thought to be dead "coming back to life". Even today there are morticians who can attest to such occurrences. The truth is that these people were not really dead. They were thought to be dead because they appeared not to be breathing and they appeared to have no pulse. Have you ever watched an old lady sleeping? She can be sleeping so peacefully that you may think she is dead. Her pulse is ever so slow, her breath ever so shallow. Her chest does not heave. Her heart seems not to throb. Does that make her dead? No.

There is one sure way to know absolutely beyond doubt when the human body is dead – it does not bleed. It cannot bleed. There is no heart beat to pump the blood. So if you cut or stab a dead body only water or lymphatic fluid will escape from the cut - no blood. Remember this when you read chapter sixteen.....dead men don't bleed.....

Chapter Fifteen

The box

Sixty years after that little boy coloured the picture with "wrong" colours he was more convinced than ever that he was right.

Now there was one difference. It had taken him sixty years to learn that *they* too were right. You see there is no wrong. God is almighty. He is omnipotent. He is omnipresent. This being so there can be no wrong. There can only be different degrees of right. It is how we see things that determine their righteousness. What we need to understand and to acknowledge is that things are as we see them. If others see them differently then so be it. It is not for us to judge. If people put us in boxes, let them. It is their boxes, not ours. The chains that we have chosen confine us only, not others. The cross that we bear is of our own making.

Having finally realized this one great truth I was free. I started my own business and it was a success. I never looked back. My family life improved dramatically. My social life was good. My health improved and as my doctor said: "You are in good shape for a man of your age." Oh yes, "a man of your age!" We all grow old. It is my wish that we may all do so gracefully. It is also my wish that we may leave this earth without any regrets.

Before laying down my head for its final rest I would like to share with you what really happened after the cross.

This knowledge came to me during the years that I ran my own business. Although being in charge of one's own business does put one under a lot of pressure, it also allows one to choose one's own working hours to a certain degree. I was able to decide when I needed a holiday and where to go and for how long. I was able to relax, to pray and to meditate on the great issues of life.

I did a fair amount of reading in my spare time. I read the bible in two different languages and visited Italy, France and Spain to do some research. Although I should have gone to Israel that country gives me the creeps. My wife was happy to visit Israel on my behalf. She also did Greece and a number of other Mediterranean countries. She loves travelling. It helped me a great deal as I wanted to get on with writing and I knew my health was starting to wane.

We found that much that is written in the bible and taken for granted is only hearsay. The entire New Testament was written decades after Jesus died. Many gospels were deliberately omitted by the church leaders of the time and much was changed to suit their needs.

Chapter Sixteen

The death of Jesus

And so we start to see the light.
Finally we get out of the box.
Or dare I say, we get off the cross.

What really happened on the cross and the days that followed?

Jesus was hanging on the cross and the Roman soldiers who were sent to watch over him until he died were doing their duty. Further back were Mother Mary and his sister in law, Mary the wife of Clopas. Also present were Mary Magdalene and a number of Jesus' friends and disciples all afraid to come too close because of the Roman soldiers.

On either side of Jesus there was hanging also on crosses, two sinners who like Jesus, had been condemned to death.

An almighty storm was brewing with thunder and lightning in the background. The soldiers were keen to go home and party as it was the evening of a holiday. Thus they said one to the other "Let us kill him then we can go in peace and know that our duty has been completed. We can be off early and we can drink and be merry with our friends."

You can guess they had already been into the drink by dint of the fact that they were able to grant Jesus his wish when he said "I thirst" as there was a vessel of wine at hand.

Now we know that the Roman soldiers were taught to mete out death with the sword and the exact manner in which this was done is of cardinal importance in this exposé of the death of Jesus.

One of the soldiers pierced his side with a spear and immediately blood and water came out. So they presumed that he was dead. For this reason they did not break his legs which they did with the two sinners. The reason for breaking the legs on the cross was a practical one. If left unbroken it could take days for the crucified to die. When the legs were broken the weight of the body transferred to the arms and the body slumped causing fluid to fill the lungs. This effectively caused the hanging person to drown in his own body fluids.

It was customary for the Jews to bury their dead before sunset. The following day was the Sabbath day. The Sabbath starts at sunset. As the Bible tells us it was Passover the next day and thus a holy day.

So, after this, Joseph of Arimathea (who was a disciple of Jesus in secret) asked Pilate if he may take away the body of Jesus. Pilate, believing Jesus to be dead, gave him permission. So he came and took the body of Jesus. Nicodemus also came and he brought with him large amounts of mixed aloes and myrrh. Then, according to the custom of the Jews, they gently bound the body of Jesus in strips of linen which had been treated with the customary spices.

Now it is so that nearby to the place where he was crucified, there was a garden and in the garden a new tomb in which no one had yet been buried. (In those days tombs were often prepared by the owners themselves. They were large cavities hewed into the side of the hill. This tomb was in fact owned by Joseph of Arimathea). Due to the impending storm Joseph and Nicodemus saw fit to temporarily place the body of Jesus in this tomb as the Sabbath was now at hand and no tomb had been prepared for Jesus.

It was their intention to leave him there until after the Sabbath. They intended to return, retrieve his body and to place it in a legitimate tomb.

It was customary in those times to seal a tomb with a stone at the entrance. Due to one of three possible reasons, they did not do this. Firstly there was the impending storm. Then there was the fast approaching Sabbath on which no self respecting Jew was to raise a finger to work. (Remember the story of the calf in the well?) The third possible reason why the tomb had not been sealed was that Joseph of Arimathea and Nicodemus merely rolled the stone gently in front of the tomb's entrance because they intended removing the body to a legitimate tomb for permanent burial after the Sabbath.

Now on the first day of the week, Mary Magdalene was up early as she was still grieving heavily for the loss of her beloved Jesus. (Remember that in the Jewish calendar the first day of the week follows immediately after the Sabbath.)

So she went up to the tomb to pray but when she got there she found that the stone had been moved and that the tomb was empty.

She ran and called Simon and Peter who together with another disciple were also on their way to the tomb. Mary Magdalene cried out to them that the body of Jesus had been taken away, since that was the logical answer to her for the empty tomb. Peter and the other disciple entered the tomb and on careful inspection found that the linen cloths from around his body and the handkerchief from his lead were lying there but there was no sign of Jesus. The disciples left and Mary tarried at the tomb still crying and confused. Remember that it was still rather dark. The sun had not yet risen.

As Mary wept a rustle from behind her caused her to turn around and lo and behold she saw Jesus standing there but she did not recognize him. Why not? Well, firstly it was still rather dark and secondly she certainly did not expect to see him there because she believed him to be dead.

Now comes the great revelation. Jesus was not dead! Why not? Well, as we explained the Roman soldiers were in a hurry to get their job done and off to their party. It is a well known fact that the method of killing taught to Roman soldiers of the day and age we are referring to was as follows. In order to kill from the front in battle one pierced the enemy from the soldier's right thus piercing the enemy in the stomach and hopefully forcing the sword (or spear) into his heart causing almost instant death. The reason for this method of attack was because the enemy (like the Roman soldiers) wore amour in battle but the amour covered only the front and rear, the sides were vulnerable. As the lines of infantry came to battle the soldiers would keep a line and always stab the soldier approaching on his right, not the one directly in front of him as his front armour would protect him. This piercing of the abdomen would result in water and blood pouring out on the removal of the sword. The pierced enemy would faint and in most cases die very quickly. Yet in about one out of five cases the pierced subject could cling on to life for as many as ten days but death was always inevitable.

The human bowels are highly susceptible to bacterial infection once perforated and the blood and water that left the wound in Jesus' side is sufficient evidence that his bowels had been perforated. The soldiers therefore knew that even if he were not clinically dead as they turned and left for their party, he certainly would be within a few days so they were safe, their job was done.

But Jesus was not dead. Certainly after his ordeal on the cross and after the pain and shock of the stabbing, he passed out and to all intents and purposes he appeared dead. Now remember the storm and the approaching Sabbath and the need to get him buried before the Sabbath (remember that starts at sunset). So Joseph of Arimathea and Nicodemus can be forgiven for not thinking that perhaps their hero was still alive. They had seen him hanging on the cross, had seen him receive the sour wine, had heard him effectively give up the ghost, had seen the Roman Soldiers pierce his side, had seen the blood and water come out. So what reason would they have to think him still alive? Neither of them were medical doctors. Their priority was to get his body safely entombed for the night and this they did to the best of their ability with the short time they had at their disposal.

Now imagine what happened when Jesus came round some hours later? He did what any of us would do in the same circumstances. He loosened himself from the strips of linen and spices which his friends had hurriedly wrapped round him. His next step was to seek help so he managed to push the stone at the mouth of the tomb sufficiently away to allow his escape. Again I ask you to recall that the stone was hurriedly placed in position and not sealed in the usual manner.

Also remember that there had been a storm so the stone was probably even easier to shift than may have been the case on a dry night. So even in his weakened state Jesus was able to move the stone. On the other hand perhaps this wasn't even necessary. Perhaps the rushing storm water caused the stone to slip away from the opening.

He was on his way to seek help when he saw Mary Magdelene at the entrance of the tomb.

So when Mary turned and saw Jesus, she did not recognize him. Oh misery of miseries, oh what a shame. Had she recognized him for what he was, a survivor of the cross, the world might have been a different place today. No, she would not have been able to save him. In those days the injuries he had suffered were a death warrant. Today, however, with the help of modern technology, super duper anti-biotics, emergency helicopters, the best surgeons, theatres and hospitals and emergency staff in the world, he would have had a great chance. But alas, 2000 years ago this was just not on. So when Jesus said to her "Why are you weeping?" she did not at first recognize him but when he called her by name she did recognize him. She immediately rushed off to tell the disciples hoping that they could help her. Yet she was confused because she thought that Jesus had risen from the dead. She thought she had seen a ghost.

Jesus, realizing the seriousness of his condition, kept out of sight of any possible Roman soldiers or other possible enemies that day and when evening fell he quietly made his way to the place where the disciples assembled for fear of the Jews. He entered the room and addressed them in his accustomed manner saying something like "Peace be with you." There surely is nothing strange about that!

You can imagine the consternation in that dimly lit room when he seemed to appear from nowhere and address them in his usual manner. Remember that rooms were often separated by light screens or hanging curtains. No doors. No presidential security. No electronic beams and such like to warn you of someone entering. Just in case you thought Jesus walked through the wall, it was not necessary. Also, it was not possible, because he was still a living human being in the physical body, albeit a very sick one. So just like you and I, he could not pass through solid walls, yet!

So the disciples were amazed, to say the least. Thus Jesus held up his hands so that they could see where the nails had penetrated him and he showed them his side. So even in the semi darkness of the room and because of his weakened and distraught condition, they clearly recognized him, but they too thought he was risen from the dead. Thus after passing on some of his usual words of spiritual wisdom, realizing that he was not going to be able to convince them of the fact that he was not risen from the dead, he thought it best to withdraw from their presence.

Now at this particular sitting, Thomas Didymus was not present and when the other disciples told him what had transpired he replied: "Bull dust, do you think I am an idiot? Should he appear again and I can feel the wounds in his hands and his side then I will believe." Thomas was by no means an idiot. On the contrary, he was the most scientific of the disciples and the least likely to give in to emotional whims.

Some days later Jesus did return, for he was now in desperate straits and seriously ill with infection already set in his bowels and spreading like fire into the rest of his body in the form of septicemia. He was running a high temperature. The first signs of delirium were setting in and Jesus knew the end was near. So he came to bid his friends goodbye. This time Thomas was present and indeed he did put his finger into the wounds caused by the nails in Jesus hands. Wounds which were now festering. He also felt the wound in Jesus side and he knew that he was touching a very sick man.

Having touched Jesus thus, he admitted to the other disciples that indeed this was the living Jesus, meaning living in body, while the others continued to believe they were looking at, and talking with, someone risen from the dead!

Sadly this was their last meeting for when Jesus left them this time he went to what we would today call a hospice. He went to a place of solitude where he knew he could die as an unknown, and in peace, and no longer deceive his Mary Magdalene, his disciples and the others whom he loved.

It took the Roman Catholic Church centuries to concede that Galileo was correct and the world was not flat. How long will it take this great and powerful religion who plays God with millions of innocent lives to accept that Jesus did not die on the cross?

Now I venture to ask…

Is the world flat?

Did Jesus die on the cross?

Chapter Seventeen

Reality

So John has come full circle. What starts must end. After much toil and after much searching John finally got out of the box. In his world he moved beyond the cross. Now the time has come to bury John.

Finally he is free.
Or is he?
Did Jesus die on the cross?
Is there life after death?
John does not know.
Do you?

Just one final sobering thought.

No matter what your faith or belief is, it is merely that - faith. As opposed to knowledge, faith depends on believing something about the unknown. In other words one believes a theory, something that is not proven, is not known, something that is an emotional dream. This is the foundation of all faiths throughout the world and through the ages - FAITH (not fact). Simply put

-man is afraid to die so he clings on to the hope of a life hereafter, a heaven, a nirvana, a re-union with loved ones, anything…

Sad, is it not ?

Very sad.

Bibliography and Research References

Baseman, Bob. The Holy Land

Carus, Paul. The Gospel of Budha. 1997

Ceram, C.W. Gods, graves and scholars. 1956

Chopra, Deepak. Ageless body, timeless mind

Dawood, N.J. The Koran. 1997

Motala, Dr Kassim E. Jesus is coming. 1997

New World Translation of the Holy Scriptures. 1984

Shutt, Prof Timothy. Hebrews, Greeks and Romans: foundation of western civilization

Sinclair, Andrew. Rosslyn Chapel and The Da Vinci Code

Sitchin, Zacharia. The lost realms. 1990

Tellinger, Michael. Slave Species of God. 2005

Thiering, Barbara. Jesus the man. 1992

About the Author

A Bachelor of Arts graduate of the North West University, the author did a High School Teacher's Diploma before embarking on a career in teaching.

Later he went into business. As a senior member of an International Pharmaceutical company he was also editor of their in-house magazine. He published a number of newspaper and magazine articles as well as poems in various anthologies.

He later went into business on his own account and is now a retired millionaire. While his studies and business interests took him all over the world he is essentially a family man living a quiet suburban life with his wife.

He has been happily married for forty years and has two children and four grand children. Although of South African nationally and Scottish descent he considers himself to be a child of the universe.